Hope for America

*Restoring Ageless Principles
to Education*

Hope for America

*Restoring Ageless Principles
to Education*

David A. Norris

Heartland Foundation, Inc.

Faithful Life Publishers

Hope for America
Restoring Ageless Educational Principles
Copyright © 2014 by Heartland Foundation, Inc.

Published by Heartland Foundation, Inc. chartered in Story County, Iowa in 1981. It is a 501(c)(3) tax-deductible public service organization; P. O. Box 1766, Ames, Iowa 50010 or dnorr@att.net — David A. Norris has donated his time as CEO.

This publication is a shared cooperative service. The goal is to get as many copies as possible in the hands of taxpayer parents, grandparents nationwide. America needs their help. Most will help when they find out what is being done that is so terribly wrong.

It may be possible however

to obtain a written contract to republish the entire book and add your firms name with a patriotic statement approved by Heartland Foundation, Inc. on a new back cover. See page 99 for additional details. Faithful Life Publishers will print these for you, they have the book text. Contact David A. Norris dnorr@ att.net for the contract information.

The book may be purchased direct from
Faithful Life Publishers or through booksellers.
Faithful Life Publishers
North Fort Myers, Florida 33903-1419
info@FaithfulLifePublishers.com or 888-720-0950
ISBN: 978-1-63073-064-2

Edited and printed by Faithful Life Publishers.
Printed in the United States of America, November 2014

With grateful thanks to the Founding Fathers
who, supported by their wives,
limited government for the sake of liberty.

This book is dedicated to
Americans—adults and youth,
native and foreign born.

*That we might train the young in our homes,
our schools and colleges to understand
and honor their heritage.*

"Patriotism is as much a virtue as justice, and is as necessary for support of societies as the natural affection is for the support of families. The Amor Patriae is both moral and a religious duty. It comprehends not only the love of our neighbors but millions of our fellow creatures, not only the present but of future generations. This virtue we find constitutes a part of the first character of history."

—Dr. Benjamin Rush, essay on patriotism published in 1773. He was a delegate to the Continental Congress from Pennsylvania and signed the Declaration of Independence. A devout Christian, Rush established Dickinson College in Carlisle, Pennsylvania, and served as professor of medical theory and clinical practice at the University of Pennsylvania from 1791 to 1813.

Contents

Acknowledgments

This book could not have been written without the documentation provided by reliable historians. The *Northwest Ordinance* and the Creator-based *Declaration of Independence* and *Constitution* are the basic charters for American law. The Founding Fathers were not going to be held hostage by the worldly claim of authoritarians, who imply that they have a divine right to rule. They reached beyond the failed practices of man and instituted the ageless values that make stability, liberty, and prosperity possible.

In his July 4, 1821 oration, as Secretary of State, John Quincy Adams (soon to become President) captured the foundation for American law:

> *It was the first solemn **Declaration** by a nation, of the only legitimate foundation for civil government. It was the cornerstone of the new fabric, destined to cover the surface of the globe. It demolished at a stroke the lawfulness of a government founded upon conquest. It swept away all the rubbish of accumulated centuries of servitude. It announced in a practical form to the world the transcendent truth of the unalienable sovereignty of the people. It proved that the social compact was no figment of the imagination; but a real solid and sacred bond of the social union.*

> [Emphasis per original]

Although secular militants have done great harm to the educational foundations of this nation conceived in liberty, there is reason for optimism. There were traitors within when the *Declaration of Independence* was adopted by Congress; yet we prevailed in the war against King George III of England.

Commendable resources that were very helpful include—
- *Understanding the Constitution* by David Gibbs, Jr.

- WallBuilders' material provided by historian, David Barton.

- A special thank you to Phyllis Schlafly (who has a superb background in the law) for her book, *Supremacists: The Tyranny of Judges and How to Stop It.*

Also, I am indebted to—
- James H. Hutson, formerly a professor of history at Yale University and now chief of the Manuscripts Division, Library of Congress

- Judge Robert H. Bork, whose office encouraged this writing on the subject of education

- Linda Waters, school teacher and author

- Dr. Lowell Bond, retired physician

- Douglas Gamble, retired manager, print shops, U.S. government worldwide

- Richard Howell, project manager, agricultural equipment manufacturer

- Dr. James Magee, agricultural services

- John Olson, retired newspaper editor

- Others (too many to list here) are cited in the book.

The public is becoming more aware that something has gone very wrong in government public school classrooms. Hope for restoring the ageless principles of education is growing.

It was my privilege to chair a Grand Jury study on problems in higher education. This occurred at the time when radicals had been given unwise tenure privileges, which made it virtually impossible to replace them.

American history has been a constant companion throughout our family's history, which began in America in 1654 with Nicholas Norris. Several family members served in the war for independence. At least one was at Valley Forge. Three did not return—exactly what happened is unknown. Four of our grandsons are in the military. The youngest completed a tour as a guard at the Tomb of the Unknown Soldier, Arlington National Cemetery. I served two years as a non-combatant during the Korean Conflict.

Endless thanks go to my dear wife, Carlene, whose love and encouragement are of inestimable value. Also, I am grateful for the help of our gifted daughters, Sharon and Sara.

Introduction

Hope for America is real and powerful. There is no denying that determined enemies of liberty are on the move and that our weakness is their hope.

By proceeding as the Community Alert Committees did in 1775, '76, and '78 and restoring education, which is central to American greatness, we can be victorious. Documenting the hope provided by that strategy is the purpose of this book. The education for American exceptionalism was briefed by Abraham Lincoln in his Second Inaugural Address, March 4, 1865.

Lincoln Memorial Statue

President Lincoln took the oath of office and then spoke to thousands of spectators standing on the Capitol grounds. A portion of that message is carved in garnet on the walls of the Lincoln Memorial. He emphasized God fourteen times and quoted the Bible twice. Lincoln concluded by saying,

> *With malice toward none, with charity for all, with firmness in the right as God gives us to see the right, let us strive on to finish the work we are in...*

Lincoln's message fills the education gap of our day. Wisdom from the Bible enables liberty to prevail over secularism, because it is both foundational and practical.

> *Trust in the Lord with all thine heart; and lean not unto thine own understanding. In all thy ways acknowledge Him, and he shall direct thy paths*
> (Proverbs 3:5-6)

Americans focused upon the conspicuously self-evident Laws of Nature and of nature's God. It is the governing character of these principles (laws), such as the Golden Rule and the Ten Commandments, which led to success. This is the foundation upon which man's right to *life, liberty and the pursuit of happiness* rests. Known as virtue, it reflects the impartial and divine element that frees man to do what is right.

> *Where the Spirit of the Lord is, there is liberty.*
> (2 Corinthians 3:17)

This book does not try to list the many names used to identify the enemies of citizen self-rule and liberty. They all have two things in common—

- They assume the authority that belongs to creation's God.

- They reject the people's God-given right to make informed decisions.

Knowledge of the equal station, to which the Laws of Nature and of nature's God entitle them, has strangely disappeared from the lexicon of public education. William Blackstone's *Commentaries on the Laws of England* were used by Abraham Lincoln and continued to be used by students of the law into the 1920s. Blackstone said,

> *Man, considered as a creature, must necessarily be subject to the laws [principles] of his Creator ... These laws laid down by God are the eternal immutable laws of good and evil ... This law of nature dictated by God himself, is of course superior in obligation to any other. It is binding over the entire globe, in all countries, and at all times: no human laws are of any validity if contrary to this.*

This *Hope for America* handbook has been published so people can understand and appreciate the truth about the culture that enabled America to be an exceptional nation. Proof that the Judeo-Christian heritage has been the primary contributor for character development in public education is overwhelming. Prior to the leftist takeover of the National Education Association and local teacher union affiliates, the NEA published God-honoring booklets for students. *A Golden Treasury from the Bible,* Personal Growth Leaflet Number 22, was published in 1950. It contained 24 Bible verses, including Psalm 1;

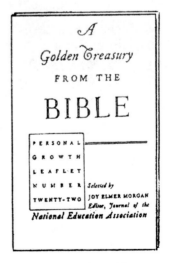

Proverbs 20:1; Exodus 20 (the Ten Commandments); Romans 12; John 3:16, 6:23, 14:1-4 and 15:1-4; 1 Corinthians 13; and Ecclesiastes 12:1. Ecclesiastes 12:1 reads, *Remember now thy Creator in the days of thy youth.*

The **In God We Trust** worldview has been the foundation for public education, from the beginning continuing for over 340 years. The Supreme Court's ruling, in the *Everson v. Board of Education* decision of 1947, began a shift toward the imperial rule of a militant secular minority. We will review the American civic religion adopted by immigrants from around the world in Chapter 4. The strategy for restoring competition in education and choice by the people is outlined in Chapters 10 through 12. Chapter emphasis is interrelated, so repetition of common values was important.

Dwight Eisenhower

Legislation drafted by the United States Senate and House of Representatives, adding the words *Under God* to the American Pledge of Allegiance, was signed by President Eisenhower in 1954. In 1964, the Supreme Court rejected a challenge to the law.

Renewed appreciation and understanding of this priority is our most powerful weapon. Americans need not be enslaved for lack of knowledge. It is the light of truth that fortifies the minds of men and women, boys and girls. We believe in them because they reflect the unrelenting power of creation's God.

Chapter 1

Americans Have Been So Blessed

America's founders had their politics right. They demonstrated a remarkable understanding of history. Americans rejected political appeals to man's lower nature, greed, fraud, countless prejudices, and addictions. Choosing the higher authority of creation's God, they strengthened families, community togetherness, and education for successive generations. This chapter includes the strategy and a plan, based upon reliable expectations and solid reasons for hope restored. Absolutes for government do exist.

Far from being secular, all aspects of human endeavor (including government) fall under the purview of creation's God. The value system for determining the proper role of laws and the use of government power is clear. *We ought to obey God rather than men.* (Acts 5:29)

Americans have been blessed because they upheld the ageless principles—

> *... that all men are created equal, that they are endowed by their Creator with certain unalienable Rights, that among these are Life, Liberty and the pursuit of Happiness.--That to secure these rights, Governments are instituted*

1

among Men, deriving their just powers from the consent of the governed.

Morality is the backbone for the rule of law. Those who advocate absolutes (such as, thou shall not steal, murder, or tell lies) are not prudes. It is the secular enemies of the traditional family, citizen self-rule, and limited government, who have gone bonkers.

Tenured secular militants, inclined to attack good teachers who support Biblical morality and the traditional family, are secure in their jobs. They represent perhaps no more than three percent of the teachers. Consequently, administrators hired by the people to run the schools are powerless to correct the problem. This appears to be directly related to the harmful teacher tenure guarantees and collective bargaining laws. The people's chain of control over what new generations will be taught has been disrupted. This is documented later.

Citizen rebellions against the tyranny of big governments have been common throughout history. Historians interested in momentous events that reversed government tyranny turn to the *Magna Carta*, 1215. The *Magna Carta* was a contract for constitutional law imposed by the people's representatives and signed by King John. The American *Constitution* was likewise a written contract for limited government agreed upon by the people. Citizen rebellions against oppressive governments also include the Great Reformation that began in 1517, the English *Bill of Rights*, 1689, and the American *Declaration of Independence* from the King of England on July 4, 1776.

The strength needed by the people to restore and maintain a representative republic have one thing in common—they were powered by a spiritual revival. On this subject Abraham Lincoln said,

What constitutes the bulwark of our own liberty and independence? It is not our frowning battlements, our bristling seacoasts, the guns of our war steamers, or the strength of our gallant and disciplined army. These are not our reliance against a resumption of tyranny in our fair land. **Our reliance is in the love of liberty which God has planted in our bosoms.** *Our defense is in the preservation of the spirit which prizes liberty as the heritage of all men, in all lands, everywhere. Destroy this spirit, and you have planted the seeds of despotism around your own doors.*

Lincoln's speech
Edwardsville, Illinois
September 11, 1858

Constitutional tests and checks against subversion alerted society to the deceptive charms advanced by authoritarian rulers. In 1779 John Adams (America's second president) and father of John Quincy Adams (our sixth president) expressed it this way, "America was a government of laws, and not of men." The *government of laws* rests upon Bible knowledge, a conscience that alerts individuals to evil behavior, and the historical record of cause and effect.

Upon the recommendation of John Adams, George Washington served as Commanding General of the Continental Army. From 1775 to 1783, the eight-year War for Independence from authoritarian rule was waged. The victory was a monumental achievement that cannot easily be explained.

American historian Sydney E. Ahlstrom credits ministers from various evangelical denominations for supporting the Great Awakening that began in the 1730s. Bible Churches were voicing the principles of the *Declaration of Independence* hundreds of years before the

Declaration was written. Although openly denied by educators and the media on the left, political freedom for churches is American. (For churches and political freedom, search Google.) There is even what was called the "black regiment." This refers to ministers who served valiantly in the American War for Independence.

The signers of the *Declaration of Independence* pledged their lives, their fortunes, and their sacred honor. Of the 56 signers, five were captured by the British as traitors and tortured; twelve had their homes ransacked and burned; two lost their sons serving in the Revolutionary Army; and another had two sons captured. Nine of the 56 fought and died from wounds or hardships in the Revolutionary War. In spite of the suffering, not one of the Founding Fathers ever reneged on his commitment to independence.

Higher Authority American charters include the *Northwest Ordinance*, the *Declaration of Independence*, and the *Constitution* (U.S. and State). They are bold American rejections of the historical rule of man. Those who do not understand their heritage as Americans, may not appreciate the importance of trust in creation's God. They may not realize the power for good provided by the Judeo-Christian Scripture. Happiness, man's highest aspiration, is not driven by coercion or tyranny of the mind, but by respect for the Creator of life and His protection.

> *For ye have been called unto liberty; only use not liberty*
> *for an occasion to the flesh, but by love serve one another.*
> (Galatians 5:13)

Creation's God gave man the freedom to choose. He is there to help those who humbly place their trust in Him. We can turn our affections toward the all-knowing Creator of life, who loves us more than we love ourselves—or follow our lower nature that Satan and his workers seek to employ. Satan is the Father of lies. Paul's focus was light in a dark world. (Philippians 2:5-16)

> *But Jesus beheld them, and said unto them, With men this is impossible; but with God all things are possible.*
> (Matthew 19:26)

> *If my people, which are called by my name, shall humble themselves, and pray, and seek my face, and turn from their wicked ways; then will I hear from heaven, and will forgive their sin, and will heal their land.*
> (2 Chronicles 7:14)

Humility replaces rebellion against God. Moral faith, supported by humble trust in God, is key to instituting the ageless principles which uphold decency for family and community. Except for being a general encourager, Constitutional law wisely prohibits government officials from establishing a church, education, or the press. This is because of the ever-present desire of some in government, to use the public treasury to control political thought by establishing education, religion, and the media. **With government establishment comes police power.** The lesson of history is, with that power, exploitation by tyranny over the minds of the people is a foregone conclusion.

Healthy religious, education, and media content comes with the freedom of the people to debate priorities and to choose. This freedom is the sacred right of parents, grandparents, and the general public— to establish their ideological priorities and then support like-minded schools, churches, and news providers.

That said, the backbone of American charters is moral law powered by the citizen's knowledge and faith in God.

5

For the first [now over 340 years] of this country's history, religion and education were intimate and interdependent. Religious competition does stir controversy, but religious freedom enriches rather than impoverishes public policy and the education process.

Edward Scott Gaustad
A Religious History of America
Harper and Row, 1966, p. 372
(Gaustad was a Professor of History
at the University of California, Riverside)

Most American leaders were not committed to Christian ministries; but because of their knowledge of the Bible and reliable renditions of history, their judgment (as laymen) was exceptional. As true statesmen, they filtered the shifting principles of worldly philosophy through the grid of Scripture.

Washington disagreed with one of the Constitutional delegates who suggested compromise for political expediency. He cautioned, that regardless of whether or not, the states would adopt a new *Constitution*.

Popular fallacies must be avoided. Let us raise a standard to which the wise and honest can repair; the event is in the hand of God.

Hamilton Abert Long
The American Ideal of 1776
Philadelphia: Heritage Books, Inc., 1963
pgs. 205–206

The fact that education in America (which supported character development) has been denigrated and reversed by secular revisionist is inescapable. God blessed America because parents and guardians who knew what was best for their children controlled what their children were taught.

Americans set the pace for greatness. Radicals in education and the media, who charge that America is an evil nation, do great harm. Yes, it took many years to implement the right of all adult citizens to vote and to liberate slaves. Americans, however, never abandoned those hard to achieve societal corrections called for in our charters at the very beginning. Let's be honest!

> *America has freed more human beings from the clutches of evil than any [other] nation on earth, and we are only a relatively young country. Even though continental Europe, in its posture of pseudo-sophistication, might consider us the country cousin of the family of nations, when these same Europeans needed to be rescued—often from themselves—we were there to rescue them. We have done it many times and in many ways, around the world. At enormous costs to ourselves, we have gone into (and out of) dozens of nations in order to make the world a better place—even those nations that were our deadliest enemies, like Germany and Japan after World War II. What MacArthur did in Japan, and what the Marshall Plan accomplished in Europe, are without historical equal, and they indicate what we think our higher calling on the planet really is! They also indicate the American penchant for forgiveness and generosity, which surpasses all others.*
>
> Dr. Jack Wheeler
> *The Ugly Liberal American*
> page 4, quoted by *The Schwarz Report*
> May 2008, Volume 48, number 5

The Spirit of Revival

The First Principle is that the God, who created man, is man's loving friend and caring helper. This is so foundational that it cannot be arrived at by any other proposition. It is the foundation upon which all other principles follow. (Philippians 4: 4-13)

The issue that confronts man is the matter of two opposing presuppositions—humble respect for the Higher Authority of creation's God, spoken of in the American *Declaration* of 1776 OR the pride of believing that men are gods unto themselves, glorified in secular humanist manifestoes. Visible in history, one is the presupposition that leads to lasting success, the other leads to confusion that ends in tyranny. The source of the problem is Satan, the Father of lies, who gained access to the mind of man described in the book of Genesis in the Hebrew-Christian Bible.

It is the impartial, omnipotent God of creation who put the miraculous complex of life together. He alone can provide the knowledge needed by man to win over Satan and his hosts. *In God We Trust* empowers believers to police their own lives. When that happens, harmful cultural outcomes are minimal and the reason for big government bosses is averted.

On March 11, 1792, George Washington explained:

> *I am sure there never was a people who had more reason to acknowledge a Divine interposition in their affairs than those of the United States; and I should be pained to believe that they have forgotten that Agency which was so often manifested during our revolution, or that they failed to consider the omnipotence of that God who is alone able to protect them.*

8

The wealth that Americans have created by employing Christian values for faith and family exceeds, by far, that of all other nations. European nations now practicing Old European secular philosophy are moving below mediocrity. In Chapter 6 we cite the history of the Soviet Socialist Empire to illustrate that those who reject the Laws of Nature and of nature's God are doomed to failure. The worldwide, multiple pronged Russian efforts to make socialism work were unprecedented.

Reading the book *Reminiscences and Reflections* by Raisa Gorbachev, wife of Mikhail Gorbachev, leader of the Soviet Union, makes the point. Raisa and Mikhail's standard of living was way below the American poverty standard, until he reached the top echelon of Soviet authority. Raisa wrote, *Our society has set out on the path of renewal and of demolishing totalitarianism and the obsolete command system of administering the country.*

> *Erase all thought...and fear of God, [fear of the boundaries provided by creation's God to protect us from ruining our own life] from a community, and selfishness and sensuality would absorb the whole man. Appetite knowing no restraint...man would trample in scorn on the restraints of human laws. Virtue, duty and principle would be mocked and scorned as unmeaning sounds. A sordid self-interest would supplant every feeling, and man would become ...a companion of brutes.*

> William Ellery Channing, 1820,*The Great Doctrine of Retribution: The Founders' Views of the Social Utility of Religion* cited by historian James H. Hutson at the American Enterprise Institute, 1150 Seventeenth Street NW, Washington, DC
> June 6, 2000

Traditional education standards see to it that students learn about the American God-honoring foundations. That elementary phase of education is the enemy of big government imperialist. Desirable knowledge, *In God We Trust*, liberates man from tyranny.

Chapter 2

Protection of Creation's God Versus the Tyranny of Man-made Law

Government is simply a tool. The power for good or bad in society rests with the people. When properly tailored that tool supports man's options, which advance what is good and discourages those lower nature choices that harm individuals, communities, and nations. Washington aptly wrote, *Government is not reason; it is not eloquent; it is force. Like fire, it is a dangerous servant and a fearful master.* (best-quotes-poems.com/George-Washington.html)

The law for government has been defined as *a set of rules for conduct prescribed by a controlling authority and having binding legal force.* (*Black's Law Dictionary,* http://en.wikipedia.org/wiki/ Black's Law Dictionary) The overriding concern is: What are the beliefs of the controlling authority? Sadly, some public servants, including the vain professors, do not respect the fact that government gets its power from the sovereigns—the taxpayers who created the government and pay their salaries.

What sets the American *Constitution* form of government apart from those of so many other nations, is that its use is rooted in the Higher Authority Judeo-Christian tradition for civil order. The *Constitution*

11

as a tool is composed of directives, checks, and obstacles. When the principles of the Creator-based *Declaration* articulated in the *Bill of Rights* are upheld, the obstacles built into the *Constitution* become morally effective. It then becomes difficult for government employees to empower a partisan political agenda and line their pockets with taxpayers' money.

There Are Two Forms of Government

Three generations ago, high school graduates would have understood the big divide, the common issue with governments throughout human history. That divide is illustrated by two approaches to the law.

> *Government is frequently and aptly classed under two descriptions, a **government of FORCE** [arbitrary and changeable rule by man-made decrees], and a **government of LAWS** [Reliable governments derive their just powers from the consent of the governed and citizens who police their own actions according to life-and community-honoring standards such as the Ten Commandments]; the **first** is the definition of despotism, the **last** Liberty.*

> Alexander Hamilton
> *Tully Papers*, 1794

Paraphrasing George Washington in his *Farwell Address*—the contract for a *Constitution* agreed to by the people, can only be changed from the original with amendments by the people themselves. Supremacist law professors have tragically rejected this truth. We now see the colossal mess that our nation is in, because of their disrespect for Constitutional law. This is a violation of both **government by law** and **citizen representative government**. When the *Constitution* is ignored, **governments of force** by strong-headed men are inevitable. Desirable **government of law** can be traced by doing a search of the words *elect, shall not*, and *our Lord* found in the U.S. *Constitution*.

How, then, can the people protect themselves from cavalier authoritarians, who manipulate changes in laws which enable them to dumb down students—and, by extension, over time manipulate society? Historians Will and Ariel Durant pointed out Solon of Athens' recognition of the critical procedural choice, that is directly related to limiting the options for political deception. Do we insist upon *government by written and permanent law*, or do we permit *government by incalculable and changeable decrees*?

George Washington in his Farewell Address reminded future generations that they cannot neglect the personal responsibility for upholding the moral predicate for law.

> *It is easy to foresee, that from different causes and from different quarters, much pains will be taken, many artifices employed, to weaken in your minds the conviction of this truth ('keep alive the spirit of Liberty'); as this is the point in your political fortress against which the batteries of internal and external enemies will be most constantly and actively directed.*

best-quotes.com/George-Washington.html

Government of laws is not complicated. No matter what one's religion, birthright, or political view, the principles of the *Declaration of Independence* and universal absolutes recorded in this book, clearly distinguish right from wrong.

Stealing property that belongs to another is violating an unalienable right upon which liberty depends. Adultery is a violation of the sacred obligations of marriage and family. It creates stress and shortens life. Dishonesty cheats the victim out of an unalienable, God-given right and undermines the reliable communication upon which commerce and community depend. Deliberately stopping the heart of an unborn child is a horrific offense to the God of life, as well as to society.

The purpose of American government is spelled out in the preamble.

> ***We the People*** *of the United States, in Order to form a more perfect Union, establish Justice, insure domestic tranquility, provide for the common defense, promote the general welfare,* [meaning common needs that do NOT conflict with the development of the work ethic and personal self-reliance] *and secure the Blessings of Liberty to ourselves and our Posterity, do ordain and establish this Constitution for the United States of America.*

The American system of government is *a Republic—a federation, or combination, of central and state republics—under which: the different governments will control each other, ...Within each republic there are two safeguarding features: (a) a division of powers, as well as (b) a system of checks and balances between separate departments [including the judiciary]: hence a double security arises [essential] to the rights of the people.* (*Federalist*, No. 51, James Madison)

As citizens, it is important to see American government in the context of the big picture. The Federal and State Republics share sovereignty, all of which is subordinate to the people. It is the exclusive right of the citizens, as sovereigns under God, to determine the functions of the separate departments and the limit of the use of government power.

14

On every question of construction, carry ourselves back to the time when the Constitution was adopted, recollect the spirit manifested in the debates, and instead of trying what meaning may be squeezed out of the text, or invented against it, conform to the probable one in which it was passed.

June 12, 1823, Thomas Jefferson,
Autobiography Notes on the State of Virginia,
Public and Private Papers, Addresses and Letters,
New York: The Library of America, 1984

Chief Justice Marshall's legal philosophy has been twisted by liberals to leverage their totalitarian rule of man philosophy. Justifying the *Marbury v. Madison* opinion, Marshall stated:

This original and supreme will [of the people] organizes the government, and assigns, to different departments, their respective powers. It may either stop here; or establish certain limits not to be transcended by those departments. The government of the United States is of the latter description. The powers of the legislature [as well as the judiciary and the administrative] are defined, and limited; and that those limits may not be mistaken, or forgotten, the Constitution is written.

(http://usa.usembassy.de/etexts/democrac/9.htm)

———————

Today's conservatives and moderates strongly object to those who force a God-rejecting Darwinian life view on our youth. Secular academies that claim Darwin's God-rejecting theory for the meaning,

15

purpose, and origin of life to be hard science, are dead wrong. Liberals who do everything they can to destroy the reputation and carrier of those who teach traditional American values are the problem.

The idea that life developed over hundreds of millions of years by a series of helpful accidents is irrational. It takes a lot more faith to believe that, than it takes to believe in the God of creation. A point in fact, the human brain is a miracle. The brain has many regions *that are connected by some 100,000 miles of fibers called white matter—enough to circle the Earth four times. Images...taken at the Martinos Center, revealed for the first time the specific pathways underlying cognitive functions.* (*National Geographic Society Magazine*, February, 2014, p.34)

God-rejecting faith in millions of years of accidents could not create a jet airplane—let alone life. It makes more sense to believe that God made man with the capacity for reasoning— thus, man is able to construct jet airplanes.

The Bible tells us that man was created some 6,000 years ago, but believers do not claim that event to be science. Scripture emphasizes the importance of humility and placing one's faith in creation's God, not slogans or pagan religion.

Dr. Soren Lovtrup, a non-Biblicist scientist, declares...*that one day the Darwinian myth will be ranked the greatest deceit in the history of science.* (Dr. Soren Lovtrup, *Darwinism: The Refutation of a Myth*, New York: Croom Helm, 1987, p. 422)

On August 5, 2014, a Des Moines Register article confronts the absurdity of Darwin's religious and scientific theory head-on. The report estimates that erosion caused by heavy rain that spring caused a loss of 15 million tons of soil in Iowa. It occurred even though farmers promote soil conservation for better yields. Those who teach that it took tens of millions of years to bring life into existence, do not seem to understand that by then, the earth would be little more than potholes, rocks, and water.

Honesty suggests that Darwinian science be subjected to religious competition and the reality of agronomic outcomes. If secular dreamers could comprehend this, they would either change what they teach or, if being honorable, they would establish and fund their own private schools. Public school teachers could again implant the values that support the traditional family and limited government.

Editors of the book, *Speeches that Changed the World,* started with the Ten Commandments (Exodus 20:1–17) and Christ's Sermon on the Mount (Matthew 5–7). These editors recognized the good that believers have contributed to society and the superior quality of the Bible as literature.

Later, in *Speeches that Changed the World,* are speeches by two Darwinian evolutionists, Adolf Hitler and Joseph Stalin. Their leadership did influence the world. The murder of millions of innocent people demonstrates the depths to which the open-mindedness of Darwin's *Origin of the Species* dogma can take man.

During the controversy over the French Revolution (which provided the evil pattern for socialism in Russia), Edmund Burke wrote this about moral education and political truth:

> *We know that we have made no discoveries; and we think*
> *that no discoveries remain to be made in morality; nor*
> *many in the great principles of government, nor in the*
> *idea of liberty, which were understood long before we*
> *were born, altogether as well as they will be after the*

grave has heaped its mould upon our presumption, and the silent tomb shall have imposed its law on our pert loquacity.

In response to the question, "What is liberty?" he stated, "Mere liberty without other forces working in the sphere that it opens up is only another name for license." (Edmund Burke's *Reflections on the Revolution in France*, 1790, London: Henry G. Bohn, 1864 extract, p. 129)

Dr. I. L. Kandell, a refugee from Romania and professor at Columbia University, aptly lamented education devoid of established knowledge, calling it *the most Communist feature of the Communist Revolution and the most Nazi expression of the National Socialist Revolution.* (I. L. Kandell, extensive studies of educational systems around the world)

When textbook writers and teachers imply that the use of moral absolutes in education is a violation of separation of church and state, they have perverted the truth. Those who force Darwin's God-rejecting origin and purpose of life religion on students' minds are using the same evil religo-education state monopoly they claim to oppose.

Judge Robert H. Bork observed that the courts, especially the Supreme Court, have become *the enemy of traditional culture*, in areas including *speech, religion, abortion, sexuality, welfare, public education and much else.* He continued, *It is not too much to say that the suffocating vulgarity of popular culture is in large measure the work of the Court.* (Jeffrey Rosen, "Obstruction of Judges," *The New York Times*, August 11, 2002)

Chapter 3

Universal Principles in Divine Law for Government Do Exist

The people come together to form a government and fund the public treasury that give it power. Portrayals of the moral absolutes for civil and criminal law are prominently displayed on the Supreme Court building in America's capital city. Revisionist pathfinders naturally appeal to man's selfish nature. To succeed they must keep the Biblical message of the Ten Commandments for law out of the courthouses and education.

Roger Williams established the American standard for hopeful immigrants throughout the world. A devout Christian and governor of Rhode Island, he instituted freedom for competition (which is a Judeo-Christian teaching) between the several religious denominations. This freedom was later made constitutional law by the First Amendment.

 The Bible tells man a truth about spiritual matters and the history of cause and effect. Now documented, political scientists tell us that the greatest single source of political inspiration for the framers of the *Constitution* was the Bible. Some

34% percent of all ideas referred to directly by the delegates came from the Old and New Testament books. Furthermore, 60% of the references to opinions of Montesquieu, Blackstone, and Locke were drawn from the Bible. The most frequently quoted book was from Deuteronomy in the Old Testament. (Professor Donald S. Lutz, *The Origins of American Constitutionalism*, Louisiana State University Press, 1988)

The official American motto, *In God We Trust*, was adopted in 1956. It replaced the *E Pluribus Unum* motto, adopted when the Great Seal of the United States was created in 1782. With that motto, the American *Constitution* was adopted on September 17, 1787 by the Constitutional Convention in Philadelphia. The *Constitution* was ratified by conventions in eleven states and went into effect on March 4, 1789.

In God We Trust is a reflection of the Creator-based *Declaration of Independence* and *Constitution*. Abraham Lincoln emphasized the Creator-based *Declaration* as the moral predicate for Constitutional law. One of the greatest messages ever delivered in America, the *Gettysburg Address* begins *Fourscore and seven years ago* [referring to the *Declaration of Independence*] *our fathers brought forth on this continent, a new nation, conceived in Liberty, and dedicated to the proposition that all men are created equal.* (Abraham Lincoln's *Gettysburg Address*, November 19, 1863)

President Harry S. Truman emphasized the ageless principles for education and law:

> *The fundamental basis for this nation's law was given to Moses on Mount Sinai. The basis of our Bill of Rights comes from the teachings in Exodus, Matthew, Isaiah, and Paul. If we don't have a proper fundamental moral background, we finally end up with a totalitarian government...*

20

President Harry S. Truman,
address before the Attorney General's Conference
on Law Enforcement Problems, February 1950

One of the beautiful boasts of our municipal jurisprudence is that Christianity is a part of the Common Law. ... There never has been a period in which Common Law did not recognize Christianity as lying at its foundations. Harvard and many other law schools eventually switched to secular based case law, leading to removal of the moral absolute's test and to what the Solon of Athens described as government by incalculable and changeable decrees. Knowledgeable citizen juries, however, take the traditional Common Law morality stand, unless prohibited by the judge's chosen statute when instructing the jury. *I verily believe Christianity necessary to the support of civil society.* (Joseph Story: U. S. Supreme Court Justice, *American Jurist and Law Magazine,* April 9, 1833, 346-48)

The **rule of law** standards include the parameters for civil behavior provided by the Ten Commandments (Exodus 20 and Deuteronomy 5). Prior to the emergence of supremacist judges, who embraced the intolerance of the secular **rule of man**, the **morality test** guided lawmakers. Up until then, government public schools emphasized the Commandments.

In Chapter 6 of this book, there is a citation pointing to **the fact that opposition to murder, theft, perjury and adultery, etc. is universal in human societies worldwide.** The willingness of law schools to mislead students into **abandoning the morality test** is astounding. Leaders entrusted by citizens to police law school curriculum made a very, very foolish mistake. Already apparent from daily news reports, if not corrected, removal of the morality test from court decisions will soon destroy civil liberty in America.

Is it any wonder that the Bible is the most sought after book throughout history? The right of new generations to be taught this truth is a sacred right!

1. Honor the One God, man's loving Benefactor and Creator. Men, driven by superstition, worshipped countless numbers of gods at the time these truths were given to us. This God is not denominational, but is the God of all creation.

Sculpture in the Supreme Court

2. Have no substitute gods. Humility and respect are important virtues for both the citizen and community.

3. You shall not take the name of the Lord your God in vain. Uphold and honor God's name.

4. Honor your parents for their role.

5. Do not murder. This reflects mankind's right to life and liberty.

6. Do not commit adultery. The sanctity of marriage between one man and one woman is an important example for children.

7. Do not steal. This protects the work ethic, the right to property ownership, and commerce.

8. Do not tell lies or testify falsely about the reputation of others. Failure to be truthful is a rejection of justice before the law.

9. Thou shalt not covet thy neighbor's house, thy neighbor's wife, nor his man servant, nor his ox, nor anything that is thy neighbors. This reflects the right to ownership, the sanctity of marriage, moral absolutes, and the family's right to privacy.

The outcomes associated with these protective Commandments are a vivid contrast to the outcomes of secular dictates that appeal to man's lower nature—which advances the destructive **political correctness** agenda.

Chapter 4

Moral Absolutes Embedded in the Declaration of Independence

By far the most consequential charter for government throughout all history is the *Declaration of Independence.* Referring to the *Declaration,* one scholar writes, "Everything in the colonial period led up to it and everything afterward flowed from it."

James Wilson

James Wilson was one of six men who signed the *Declaration of Independence* and the *Constitution of the United States.* His contribution to the deliberations of the *Constitution* was second only to James Madison's. Addressing the Pennsylvania Ratifying Convention for the new constitution, Wilson stated, "I beg to read a few words from the *Declaration of Independence* made by the representatives of the United States and recognized by the whole Union."

We hold these truths to be self-evident, that all men are created equal, that they are endowed by their Creator

> *with certain unalienable Rights, that among these are Life, Liberty and the pursuit of Happiness. — That to secure these rights, Governments are instituted among Men, deriving their just powers from the consent of the governed, — That whenever any Form of Government becomes destructive of these ends, it is the Right of the People to alter or to abolish it, and to institute new Government, laying its foundation on such principles and organizing its powers in such form, as to them shall seem most likely to effect their Safety and Happiness.*

Wilson concluded, "This [*Declaration*] is the broad basis on which our independence [from authoritarian rule] was placed; on the same certain and solid foundation this [the *Constitution of the United States*] system is erected." (Cited in John Elliot, *Elliot's Debates, The Debates in the Several State Conventions Adoption of the Federal Constitution*, Philadelphia, Pennsylvania 11-20-1787, Book I, published 1836, p. 457)

Called America's Civic Religion, the *Declaration of Independence* was adopted unanimously by the Continental Congress on July 4, 1776.

American Principle One:
The Spiritual Nature of Man is Supreme
All men are created . . . endowed by their Creator...
—*Declaration of Independence*

American Principle Two:
God is the Source of Man's Unalienable Rights
... all men are...endowed by their Creator with certain unalienable Rights, that among these are Life, Liberty and the pursuit of Happiness.
—*Declaration of Independence*

American Principle Three:
The Traditional Family Is Paramount
The most important consequence of marriage is, that the husband and the wife become in law only one person.
—James Wilson, *Natural Rights of Marriage*, 1792

American Principle Four:
All Men Are Equal in the Sight of God and the Law
...that all men are created equal...
—*Declaration of Independence*

American Principle Five:
Liberty from Oppression by Big Government and Militant Secular Authoritarians
...unalienable Rights, that among these are...liberty.
—*Declaration of Independence*

American Principle Six:
Governments derive *their just powers from the consent of the governed.*
—*Declaration of Independence*
The sovereignty of man under God over government.
—Traditional Saying

American Principle Seven:
Moral Duties of Civility Are a Predicate for Interpreting Constitutional Intent
Tis substantially true that virtue or morality is a necessary spring of popular government. Who that is a sincere friend to it, can look with indifference upon attempts to shake the foundation of the fabric?
—George Washington's, *Farewell Address*

American Principle Eight:

The Overriding Concern When Designing the Constitution Was Checking Man's Sin-Prone Nature

The public treasury and power are tempting. *In questions of power then, let no more be heard of confidence in man, but bind him down from mischief by the chains of the Constitution.*

—*Virginia Resolutions*, Thomas Jefferson

American Principle Nine:

Authoritarians in Government Are a Parasitic And Ever-present Danger

...taking away our charters, abolishing our most valuable laws, and altering fundamentally the forms of our governments [constitutions].

—*Declaration of Independence*

American Principle Ten:

Government Must Be Decentralized

*The necessity of reciprocal checks in the exercise of political power, by dividing and distributing it into different depositories, and constituting each the guardian of the public weal against invasions by the others, has been evinced by experiments ancient and modern; **some of them in our country and under our own eyes.** To preserve them must be as necessary as to institute them.*

—George Washington, *Farewell Address*

American Principle Eleven:
Government or Union Monopolies Involving Education, Religion, Speech, or the Press Prohibited for Liberty's Sake

Congress shall make no law respecting an establishment of religion [education monopoly], or prohibiting the free exercise thereof; or abridging the freedom of speech, or of the press; or the right of the people peaceably to assemble, and to petition the Government for a redress of grievances.
—First Amendment, Constitution of the United States

The main weapons used by enemies of citizen self-rule and liberty is physical force and tyranny of the mind. Permitting the use of government power to direct behavioral, religious, social, political, and history instruction always leads to tyranny of the mind. For instance, the moral decline among our youth, that started when politicians permitted the establishment of teacher union domination, compares with the tragic church-state monopoly of Medieval Europe.

First-amendment law is superior to all other laws—national, state, and local. It is the competition of many education suppliers and religious liberty that reduces inefficiencies in government-run schools and helps restrain moral pollution by tenured government radicals.

American Principle Twelve:
Vital to American Work Ethic, Property Ownership Must Be Secure

Our wish...is, that...[there be maintained] ...that the state of property, equal or unequal, which results to every man from his own industry, or that of his fathers.
—President Jefferson, Second Inaugural Address

28

That Government is instituted and ought to be exercised for the benefit of the people: which consists in the employment of life and liberty, with the right of acquiring and using property, and generally of pursuing and obtaining happiness and safety.
—First Session of Congress in proposing *Bill of Rights* amendments to *U. S. Constitution*

American Principle Thirteen:
Government Power and Taxes Limited for Liberty's Sake
...imposing Taxes on us without our Consent...
— Declaration of Independence

Liberty and security in government depend not on the limits, which the rulers may please to assign to the exercise their own powers, but on the boundaries, within which their powers are circumscribed by the Constitution.
—James Wilson, *Lectures,* 1790

American Principle Fourteen:
Life Liberty and Happiness—Humanity's Goal
Unalienable rights, that among these are Life...and the pursuit of Happiness.
—Declaration of Independence

American Principle Fifteen:
Benevolent Provision and Heart of God for Man Recognized
*And for the support of this Declaration, with a **firm reliance on the protection of Divine Providence we mutually pledge to each other our Lives, our Fortunes, and our sacred Honor.***
—Declaration of Independence

Those teaching that Benjamin Franklin and many other Constitutional Fathers were irreligious, are teaching deceptive falsehoods. Franklin was a delegate from Pennsylvania to the second Continental Congress and signer of the *Constitution of the United States.*

Benjamin Franklin

Franklin wrote about the First Principle in his *Articles of Belief.*

I believe there is one supreme, most perfect Being . . . Also when I stretch my imagination through and beyond our system of planets, beyond the visible fixed stars themselves, into that space that is [in] every way infinite, and conceive it filled with suns like ours, each with a chorus of worlds forever moving round him; then this little ball on which we move, seems, even in my narrow imagination, to be almost nothing, and myself less than nothing, and of no sort of consequence...That I may be preserved from atheism ... Help me, O Father! For all thy innumerable benefits; for life, and reason...My good God, I thank thee!

It is not too late to restore these values. Restoring traditional education would bring these values back to American society.

Chapter 5

The Federal Constitution is a Local Citizen Control, Under God, Over Government Charter

The *Constitution* is a sovereignty of man, under God, over government contract, agreed to by the people. One of the many absolutes spelled out in the *Constitution,* that restricts the role and use of government power, is the citizen jury system. This system requires that any defendant accused of a crime be judged by local citizens, not a government judge. The jury system makes this very clear in their oath. "You, as jurors, are the judges of the facts…your sworn duty to follow all of the rules of law… so help you God." It is the citizen jury members who take this oath, and they, not a judge, decide the guilt or innocence in criminal trials brought on by the government. **No one, including the President of the United States, has the right to deny this authority--it belongs to the people.**

People of different faiths, with different racial and cultural backgrounds, who are gifted in different ways are created equal at birth and deserve to be treated equally by the civil and criminal justice systems. Any concept of authoritarianism that presumes to override the sovereignty of man, under God, over government, is a violation of *equal in the sight of God and the law.*

The multitude I am speaking of is the body of people— no contemptible multitude—for whose sake government is instituted; or rather, who have themselves erected it, solely for their own good—to whom even kings and all in subordination to them, are strictly speaking, servants and not masters.

Samuel Adams, essay in the *Boston Gazette*, 1771

In addition to the citizen jury system, the *First Amendment*, the *Tenth Amendment,* and State *Constitutions* were framed to protect local citizen control. It is at these points of constitutional law that political engineering militants and secular path finders focus their propaganda. Propaganda is information (especially false information) that an organization spreads in order to influence people's opinions and beliefs. The lesson from history is, the plans of those who denigrate the concept of the local citizen control should cause alarm. Propaganda and education shortcomings have enabled secular exclusivists to bypass local citizen authority with devastating consequences.

The Iowa *Constitution* provides an excellent portrayal of the *Declaration of Independence* for law. Iowa entered the Union as a state in 1864. Similar to other state Constitutions, Iowa provides the means for local citizen decision-making and control that is far superior to national government decision-making.

WE THE PEOPLE of the State of Iowa, grateful to the Supreme Being for the blessings hitherto enjoyed, and feeling our dependence on Him for a continuation of those blessings, do ordain and establish a free and independent government, by the name of the STATE OF IOWA.

Article I, Section 1: All men are, by nature, free and equal, and have certain inalienable rights—among which are those of enjoying and defending life and liberty, acquiring, possessing and protecting property, and pursuing and obtaining safety and happiness.

Article I, Section 2: Government is instituted [by the people] for the protection, security and benefit of the people. All political power is inherent in the people.
They [the people] have the right at all times, to alter or reform the government, whenever the public good may require it.

Article IX, Section 3 of the Iowa Constitution: The General Assembly shall encourage by all suitable means the intellectual, scientific, moral and agricultural improvement..."

Excerpts from the unanimous Grand Jury Study
of Harmful Activities in Education

The underpinning of moral absolutes for Constitutional law is as important to the survival of liberty as the 10-digit number system is essential to mathematics. Teaching that 4 x 20 = 110 would cause mathematical and scientific failure. The people's representatives in Congress do not, in the strict sense, make law. They apply pre-existing moral based laws provided by creation's God and capable of correcting starkly different problems.

Americans connected the dots.

In the chain of human events, the birthday of the nation is indissolubly linked with the birthday of the Savior. The

33

Declaration of Independence laid the cornerstone of human government upon the first precepts of Christianity.

Sixth President John Quincy Adams,
Oration on the Sixty-First Anniversary of the Creator-based
Declaration of Independence, July 4, 1837

The Most Important Constitutional Law—the First Amendment

When the *Articles of Confederation* was replaced by the new *Constitution*, the *Northwest Ordinance* was passed again and became effective under the new *Constitution*. George Washington signed the *Northwest Ordinance* back into law on August 7, 1789. Article III of the Ordinance specified that *Religion, morality, and knowledge, being necessary to good government and the happiness of mankind, schools and the means of education, shall forever be encouraged.*

During this same period of time (July 17 to August 7, 1789*), the same men who had implemented the Northwest Ordinance were writing*

Signing of the Constitution, September 17, 1787.

the First Amendment to the Constitution [prohibiting the power of government officials to interrupt religious freedom, printing press and education competition]" Historian, David Barton, *Education and the Founding Fathers*, Aledo, Texas: WallBuilder Press, 1993, p. 4.

> *Congress shall make no law respecting an establishment of religion, or prohibiting the free exercise thereof; or abridging the freedom of speech, or of the press; or the right of the people peaceably to assemble, and to petition the government for a redress of grievances.*

Sadly some secular authoritarians in government, particularly the judiciary who were misled as law students, are now living in the confusion of darkness. They are rejecting the Morality Test, upon which stability and veracity (truth or honesty) of American law was based.

The Illusion Of Reality
(Rebellion against God / incalculable and changeable decrees)

Ship Without an Anchor—Education and Laws
Waxing Worse and Worse

In Denial of Truth—
The Godless Relativistic Presupposition

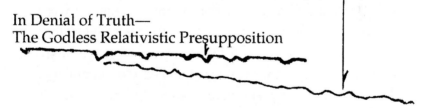

A review of the First Amendment includes five factors. All of them uphold the sacred rights of the people for equal access to competing sources of knowledge.

One: Access to informational sources for choosing qualified legislators, administrators, and school board representatives.

Two: The people and Liberty are no match for the totalitarian force. Unjust teacher contracts that eliminate the teacher's accountability to the local standards norm for civil behavior, must be reversed. When government education systems are propelled by teacher employment guarantees that are protected by the force of law, tyranny of the students' minds soon follows.

Three: Truth, when presented, can prevail by itself over non-truth. That is why secular authoritarians need the power of government monopoly education, in order to remove truth from textbooks and to confuse and manipulate the student's beliefs.

Four: When pubic education exercises the freedom for religious competition, in the context of history that was practiced for the first 340 years in America, schools will again implant the values for family, limited government, and national greatness (see pages 38-42).

Five: Unlike political monopoly union leveraging over government, imposing the atheistic secular religion for education, they have been less effective in penetrating and secularizing seminaries and churches. **God honoring churches are a very significant hope for the advance of virtue, essential for citizen self-rule, industry, and responsible liberty.**

The Judeo-Christian faith that blossomed in America is a freedom-supporting option, rather than a demanding religion or humanist authoritarianism. Families who include Bible-believing church fellowship in their activities have found:

1. The Bible provides the pattern for life that protects believers, their families, and communities from man's enemy. Satan, man's enemy, is the father of lies who gave birth to the blinding nature of man's pride spoken of in Genesis chapter three of the Bible.

2. Those who say *yes* to Jesus (believers) are forgiven and the spiritual wounds from their sin is removed.

3. There comes a noticeable spiritual capacity to make better decisions, particularly the determination to reject the old nature manipulated by Satan and his hosts. Through prayer and faith, some victims of addictive vices have been freed from the addiction.

4. God gives believers the capacity for *agape* love that empowers understanding and harmonious relationships.

5. Bible churches were teaching the principles of family solidarity, human equality, and citizen sovereignty over government under God's leadership, centuries before the *Declaration of Independence* was written.

6. Believers reject the sins of political exploitation, public warfare between genders and races, and the deceptive promises of a here and now political utopia.

The benefits of the family's involvement in a Bible-honoring church makes the demise of the traditional family and American exceptionalism less probable.

37

President George Washington, a strong Christian church man, speaking of Thanksgiving Day in 1796, invited *...the people of these States to the service of that great and glorious Being who is the beneficent author of all the good that was, that is, or that will be; that we may then all unite in rendering unto Him our sincere and humble thanks for His kind care and protection of the people of this country...* (Peter A. Lillbach, *George Washington's Sacred Fire*, Provience Forum Press, 2006, p. 271-285)

First Amendment law should prevail over ALL other amendments. Government of laws *rest[s] its authority upon the authority of that law which is Divine....Far from being rivals or enemies, religion and law are twin sisters, friends, and mutual assistants....*(James Wilson: Signer of the *Declaration of Independence,* the *Constitution,* and original Justice on the U.S. Supreme Court)

George Washington

Common law used by Abraham Lincoln helps to protect education from secular politicos. Displacing Common law that rests with moral absolutes is corrupting the judiciary. The Supreme Court majority used Case law theory in their Everson v. Board of Education decision. The Supreme Court majority changed the historical understanding of the *establishment of religion* clause of the First Amendment.

In the 1947, Judge Hugo Black wrote the Court's opinion saying this: *'establishment of religion' clause of the First Amendment means at least this: Neither a state nor the Federal Government can set up a church. Neither can pass laws which aid one religion, AID ALL*

RELIGIONS, or prefer one religion over another. Judge Black's interpretation rejected the First Amendment meaning and intent.

By adding three words, *AID ALL RELIGIONS,* Judge Black undermined the historic foundation for faith-based morality when training American youth. Reverend Joseph F. Costanzo, when quoting lecturer and author George Goldberg, a graduate of Harvard Law School, made **a prediction that proved to be true.** He called the Everson v. Board of Education ruling *the federal takeover of religion in America.* (D. James Kennedy and Norman R. Wise, *Defending the First Amendment,* 1989, TCRM Publishing, Ft. Lauderdale, Florida, 9-30)

The Everson v. Board of Education decision twisted the meaning of the First Amendment of the *Constitution* in two fundamental ways.

First, the phrase emphasizes separation of church and state—unlike the First Amendment, which speaks in terms of non-establishment and free exercise of religion. Second, a wall [term used by the Court] is a bilateral barrier that inhibits the activities of both civil government and religion—unlike the First Amendment, which imposes restrictions on civil government only not on religious freedom.

Daniel L. Dreisbach, Professor of Justice, Law, and Society at American University in Washington, D C, "How a Misused Metaphor Changed Church–State Law, Policy, and Discourse," essay, *Heritage Foundation* publication, June 23, 2006 www. heritage.org/initiatives/first-principles

1948: McCollum v. Board of Education, the court decided in favor of McCollum, an Atheist who objected to the religious classes, stating that her son was ostracized for not attending them. McCollum sued the school board, stating that the religious instruction in the public schools violated the Establishment Clause of the First Amendment The dissenting judge in this case, Stanley F. Reed, pointed out that Thomas Jefferson's use of the words, *wall of separation*, was used wrongly by the Court to support their decision.

The Court majority gutted the quality of taxpayer-funded education for decades. The inclusion of religion in education advanced by Thomas Jefferson and James Madison and adopted by the University of Virginia, calls attention to judicial imperialism. This is another example of the tragic injustice and violation of the *Constitution* caused by turning to the Case method for judging an issue, rather than applying the Morality Test of common law.

On June 17, 1963, in a Baltimore lawsuit brought by avowed atheist Madelyn Murray (later O'Hair), the judges ruled it was unconstitutional for a state to have portions of the Bible recited in schools (despite excusing anyone who wished to be excused), calling this an establishment of religion. Justice Potter Stewart, the lone dissenter, said that **the ruling had not led to true neutrality with respect to religion, but led to the *establishment of a religion of secularism.*** This decision also made it clear that prayer was banned.

In June of 1963, the Wall Street Journal commented that atheism was now *the one belief to which the State's power will extend its protection.*

Justice Anthony M. Kennedy, speaking for the nation's highest court, said, "Prayers and invocations have been a routine feature of legislatures and city councils throughout American History...The First Amendment's ban on an established religion does not require that legislative prayer may be addressed only to a generic God."

To enforce such a requirement would mean judges would have to review the prayers and 'act as censors of religious speech.' Prayer for city councils and other public boards, which was the issue before the court, are free to open their meetings with an explicitly Christian prayer, ruling that judges may not act as *censors of religious speech simply because the prayer reflects the views of the dominant faith.* [That also applies to prayer in government public schools.]

Quotes, Ames, Iowa *Tribune*
Tuesday, May 6, 2004, p. A5

The Social, Political, and Religious Atmospheres for Education Are Important

I served as the Chairman of the citizen Grand Jury for the Eleventh Judicial District of Iowa that investigated harmful activities in higher education. The Story County Attorney and District Judge had asked me to chair that Grand Jury. Three citizens each from the two major political parties and myself published a unanimous report.

We found that the athletic department was well managed. The faculty in the hard sciences, engineering, agriculture, mathematics, chemistry, physics, etc. were busy doing their work and making significant advances in the knowledge helpful to the public. The Grand Jury could not say the same about a very small segment within the soft science-related studies such as religion, history, and politics. We had recorded classroom presentations provided by the County attorney. The ever-present danger of government powered leftists' propaganda requires citizen alertness and commitment.

> *Moral, social, and political concepts implanted during the time of mental immaturity not only participate in the conduct of later life, but, once acquired, such concepts become dominant and often unalterable in the adult. Thus, captive audiences of immature minds provide powerful and much-prized forums for anti-Judeo-Christian, anti-American indoctrination. Educational environments, left unguarded, can easily be captured by alien militants, in due course, transformed into climates of unquestioned social and political opinion.*

> Grand Jury Presentment
> Harmful Activities in Education

A community's standards for public education are far superior to the statutes for law argued by lawyers, who seek to uphold a teacher's privilege to teach in violation of community standards. To say that a rebel teacher's right for what is taught is superior to citizen community authority is a totalitarian ideological doctrine. We elect school board members who agree to select a superintendent to run the school to advance the standards of the taxpayer community.

Statutes are important for the punishment of crimes, not teacher superiority over taxpayer employers. Justification for the retention of teachers, means employing only those who unequivocally encourage students to respect community values and be less likely to become criminals. Failure to do so leads to criminal acts, murder, stealing, telling lies, rape, adultery, etc. and disrespect for the laws that are needed to punish criminal acts.

Societal values acceptable to public conduct are a higher standard than criminal conduct (I Corinthians 10:23). The societal views projected by school systems are subject to the superior judgment of ordinary citizens, their school board members, and administrators employed to superintend what students are and are not taught. Everyone, including students, caught in the union web of guaranteeing the employment of teacher rebels seems to be victimized, except those teachers who do not like societal standards, the lawyers hired by the union to defend teacher misfits, and the monopoly union bosses.

Hope for America rests on two motivational fronts. First, exposing the leftists' secular revisionism causes students to lose faith in American foundations. Secondly, re-instituting the non-sectarian Judeo-Christian natural and common law for protecting public school instruction that upholds morality and history.

> We the people in this immigrant nation are against evil.
> The cure for teenage suicide is not revisionist immorality.
> The cure for poverty is not the increase of it.
> The cure for oppression is not hiding it.
> The cure for evil is not to justify it.
> The cure for injustice is not legalizing it.

School board members and administrators dismiss school bus drivers who fail to practice public safety without having to spend hundreds of thousands of dollars in lawyer fees and maybe years in appeals. The same principle should apply for the dismissal of harmful teachers who rebel against local community standards and administrative authority.

The skills required of a school superintendent for staff selection are great. The superintendent is challenged to understand the impact of relationships and the importance of retaining morality sensitive administrators and teacher assistants. The chief administrator starts with the knowledge that students, even many college students, are still in the formative stage of development and vulnerable to the deception of secular open-mindedness. A teacher in the behavioral, social, and political studies is **unqualified** if he/she fails to warn students about life practices that destroy families, personal health and civil relationships. Decision-making for school boards about school facilities, etc. is important, **but far more important should be their concern** as representatives of the citizens for decent teacher standards and selection.

Choosing teacher-selecting committee members is one of the most important duties of the superintendent. I have an acquaintance that taught in the same school for over thirty years. The superintendent put that person on the selection committee because, as he said, "Your standards are exemplary." Due diligence by teacher-selection committee members will point teacher candidates to a copy of the declining Cultural Indicator statistics printout. (See Chapter 8, pages 66-68.) This assures that the candidates understand that, if employed, they have the duty to uphold human dignity and strong family and community values. If a militant secular exclusivist gets through the gate, rebellion that hinders school administration ability to champion the sacred rights of the citizens becomes inevitable.

Dr. John Dewey, a proponent of teacher employment guarantees at taxpayer expense, is the acknowledged father of modern-day

public education. He was an admirer of Margaret Sanger, Humanist of the Year in 1967 and a founder of Planned Parenthood. Sanger also founded the publication *The Woman Rebel,* whose slogan was "No Gods! No Masters!" Her first edition denounced marriage as a *degenerate institution* and sexual modesty as *obscene prudery.* (George Grant, *Legacy of Planned Parenthood,* Wolgemuth & Hyatt, Publishers, Inc.)

**Dr. John Dewey presents Margaret
Sanger with the American Women's
Association Medal, 1932.**

Secularized education detaches new generations from the key to American greatness, *In God We Trust.* They do not want a Christmas tree to be seen by students in the halls of learning. The celebration of Christmas symbolizes the birth of the most consequential Person for good in history. *The name of the Lord* (says the Scripture) *is a strong tower; thither the righteous flee and are safe.* (Samuel Adams letter, December 26, 1776. Adams was a signer of the *Declaration of Independence*; ratifier of the U.S. *Constitution*; governor of Massachusetts)

> *A decorated pine tree in the high school cafeteria has been taken down because of complaints from a high school employee and some parents. In the words of the school principal, 'We are in the business of educating students. I didn't want this* [decorated pine tree] *to become a distraction... so we decided it would be best to take down the tree.*
>
> The *Ames Tribune,* December 4, 2010

Circumstances may prevent it, but the assistance of a conservative school board member on the teacher selection committee would add to the protection needed by students, parents, and the good teacher majority. Union contracts that prevent school board members from assisting school administrators from interviewing teacher candidates should be rejected—period.

Karl Marx championed worldwide socialism. He appealed to academia for the abolition of the family. *The bourgeois clap-trap about the family and education, about the hallowed correlation of parent and child is disgusting.* (Karl Marx and Frederick Engels, *Manifesto of the Communist Party, 1848,* http://www.anu.edu. au/polsci/ marx/ classics/manifesto.html)

Marx objected to a married man and women for several reasons. One is they are motivated to take responsibility and, if they can, to be property owners. Another, moms and dads have a heart for their offspring. They teach their children and even pay others to help teach their children to be honest, to respect creation's God, and be self-reliant. This protects them from entrapment and exploitation by socialist's propaganda.

What are professor tenure guarantees accomplishing for the education, social, political, historical, and religious studies in our universities?

"The strides made by Marxism at American universities in the last two decades are breathtaking," says New York University's Herbert London. He reports that two self-declared *Marxist historians, Eugene Genovese and William A. Williams, were elected presidents of the Organization of American Historians in successive elections. Louis Kampf, a radical with Marxist predilections, was elected president of the Modern Languages Association.* (Herbert London, Newsmax Dr. Arnold Beichman and Professor John P. Diggens echo that concern. *The field of American History has come to be dominated by Marxists and feminists.* (*Accuracy in Academia Campus Report*, July/August 1987)

Marxist academics are today's power elite in the universities. (Georgie Anne Geyer, "Marxism Thrives on Campuses," a *Denver Post* article, quoted by Arnold Beichman, August 29, 1989, p. B7)

The complexion of education in everything from genetics to sociology and psychology has become decidedly, materialistic. (Malachi Martin, "The Rising Tide of Marxists' Interpretation of History, Law, Religion and Scientific Inquiry," p. 262)

In the fall of 2005, researchers at the University of Connecticut's National Civic Literacy Board conducted a survey of some 14,000 freshmen and seniors at 50 colleges and universities. Students were asked 60 multiple-choice questions to measure their knowledge in four subject areas: America's history, government, international relations, and market economy. Seniors, on average, failed all four subjects; their overall average score was 53.2 percent. (*The Coming Crisis in Citizenship: Higher Education's Failure to Teach America's History and Institutions,* 09/26/2006, Intercollegiate Studies Institute's National Civic Board Report)

Chapter 6

The Mainstream of Progress— Education that Upholds Human Dignity and Liberty for Religious Dialogue

Secular distortions of American history are bold lies.

Truth—What the Kings of Political, Religious, and Economic Fraud Cannot Conquer

> *Of all the dispositions and habits which lead to political prosperity, religion and morality are indispensable supports. In vain would that man claim the tribute of patriotism, who should labor to subvert these great pillars of human happiness, these firmest props of the duties of men and citizens. The mere politician, equally with the pious man, ought to respect and to cherish them. A volume could not trace all their connections with private and public felicity. Let it simply be asked: Where is the security for property, for reputation, for life, if the sense of religious obligation deserts the oaths which are the instruments of investigation in courts of justice?*

> George Washington's Farewell Address, 1796,
> http://avalon.law.yale.edu/18th century/washing.asp

A detailed rejection of *The Ten Commandments on the Courthouse Lawn and Elsewhere* was written by Professor Paul Finkelman and published in a Fordham Law Review, Volume 73, Issue 4, Article 9, in 2005. Finkelman's law review thoroughly resourced the subject as far as it goes, but he did not treat the history of law in America in a credible manner.

The Professor deserves credit that many textbook writers and teachers cannot claim. **He included the fact that opposition to murder, theft, dishonesty and adultery, etc. is universal in human societies worldwide.**

The theology in many societies leads them to worship false gods, but moral standards for civility are universally held in the minds of men. Paraphrasing Webster, individuals who have not defiled their consciences have feelings, which tell him whether they are doing something that is right or wrong. When their conscience is **not defiled** (by continual school room exposure to the false religion of secularism five hours a day, nine months a year for years) respect for morality does prevail. It is the one core value that encompasses all education, law, and relationships that proves helpful.

By maintaining a clear conscience, we know what we are doing is or is not morally right. *For when the Gentiles, which have not the law, do by nature the things contained in the law, these, having not the law, are a law unto themselves.* (Romans 2:14) The Scripture continues, *Which shew the work of the law written in their hearts.*

Freedom of conscience is as much an American value for law, as the principal of human equality is a standard for justice. In Genesis 1:26, the Bible declares that man was created in the image of God.

There are slight variations of the Ten Commandments, but that does not discourage immigrant Americans from placing them where they belong—in classrooms and the courthouse. The professor seems to suggest that the Commandments be prohibited on government property, schools, courthouses, etc. because they are taught by the moral religions, which supposedly makes it a violation of First Amendment law. How foolish! Morality is universal and always prevails when applied. **It is the core human value that encompasses all education, law, and relationships that proves helpful.**

The Professor is not a liar. As a university student, he was probably the victim of the colossal fraud now being imposed on many students in lower level classrooms. Teaching distortions that twist the intent and meaning of American charters for government is advancing lies.

Worldwide terrorism is less a threat to liberty in America than the secularization of instruction in captive taxpayer-funded classrooms. Adding to the decline in vital cultural indicators, growing dishonesty and ineptitude in federal government has caused the nation's role in the world situation to become problematic.

As Justice Brandeis said, "Sunlight is the best disinfectant." (www. law.louisville.edu/library/collections/brandeis/.../196). Secular intellectuals claim to be patriots because, as they say, dissent is American. What they mean is evident from how their deception has gutted traditional American values for law and education. They demand freedom for themselves, but reject academic freedom (the freedom to be honestly informed) and the freedom of others to choose. The soft underbelly of the secular left is the fact that they cannot withstand the competition of ideas. For them, it is intolerable to allow students to learn of the *Laws of Nature and of Nature's God* that *entitle them, a decent respect…*

Few would deny that the government education system, financed by a tax on the people, is putting America to the ultimate test. We hasten to note that the problems are emphasized in two publications (highlighted below), rest with union politics and a very small percentage of teachers who are secular militants. A tenured secular minority has become sovereign within our country, over citizens and their school administrators' authority.

Are revisionist textbook writers and teacher guidelines that advocate open-mindedness in matters of moral pollution responsible for misleading tens of millions of students? *U.S. News & World Report*, states, *Many parents view the public schools as ineffective and dangerous, and are exploring the other options before it is too late.* (U.S. News & World Report, 9 December 1991. Also, the *Forbes* magazine published well-documented reports by teachers and former union leadership in *How the National Education Association Corrupts Our Public Schools,* (Brimelow, P. and L. Spencer, *Forbes* magazine, June 7, 1993)

Immigrants to America have personally experienced the coercion of force and what Thomas Jefferson called *tyranny of the mind.* The rejection of government established religion and education monopolies is the reason that millions of immigrants from different ethnic and religious backgrounds came to America. That bond is reflected in the nation's celebration of Christmas. This is validated by the *USA Today*/Gallup Poll, May, 2010: *Ninety-two percent of Americans say they believe in God and ninety-five percent approve of the National Day of Prayer.*

Schools belonging to and funded by Americans have become captive to leftist teacher union monopolies in three ways.

First: Those legislator candidates who promote the unions' political agenda, are advantaged over non-union candidates because of large campaign gifts received from unions. This allows union bosses to control legislation for teacher union contract negotiations and to impose heavy dues on teachers.

Second: School board representatives elected by the people to serve family and community interests complain that they are unable to do so, because local citizen control has been taken away from the citizens. They are correct in making that charge. (Ames, Iowa *Tribune*, January 18, 2009)

Third: The teacher majority is also captive to the liberal legislator-union boss combination. **The fear of union power among the school superintendents and good teacher majority is a factor. This fear may cause former teachers who understand what is wrong, but having union retirement plans causes them to remain quiet or even disassociate from concerned citizens.**

President Washington insisted that religion and morality were integral to education. A well-educated citizenry is absolutely essential to maintain both the law and liberty and in having the ability to distinguish between liberty and license. In other words, human dignity and civil community are not possible, if the people are ignorant. (Peter A. Lillback, George *Washington's Sacred Fire,* Providence Forum Press, 2006, p. 479)

In 1954, Congress ordered that *a room with facilities for prayer and meditation* be made available in the United States Capitol. The seventh edition of *The Capitol*, an official publication of the United States Congress, describes the stained-glass window of the Congressional Prayer Room:

The history that gives this room its inspirational lift is centered in the stained glass window. George Washington kneeling in prayer...is the focus of the composition...Behind Washington a prayer is etched: 'Preserve me, O God, for in Thee I put my trust," the first verse of the sixteenth Psalm. There are upper and lower medallions representing the two sides of the Great Seal of the United States. On these are inscribed the phrases: annuit coeptis— 'God has favored ourundertakings'— and novus ordo seclorum—'A new order of the ages is born.' Under the upper medallion is the phrase from Lincoln's immortal Gettysburg Address, 'This Nation under God.'... The two lower corners of the window each show the Holy Scriptures, an open book and a candle, signifying the light from God's law, 'Thy Word is a lamp unto my feet and a light unto my path' (Psalm 119:105)

Student understanding of this American civic religion in taxpayer-funded schools is a foremost curriculum requirement (mentioned in Chapter 4). By excluding the denominational creeds and biases that tend to be divisive, the people unify in support of governments that honor *In God We Trust* as a nonsectarian creed.

Militantly opposed by secular political correctness advocates and politicos, public school students need to be taught these traditional American character-building qualities. Students will soon be the leaders who will shape the future. Chief among the reasons for immigrating to America has been the Judeo-Christian respect for equal treatment under the law.

What is it that led to societal decay in Russia? The title of Aleksandr Solzhenitsyn's 1979 Harvard Templeton address was, "Godlessness, the First Step to the Gulag." *Creation's God made us in His image so that we can experience the depth of His love—not only with Him, but also with each other* (quote by Aleksandr Solzhenitsyn, the great Russian historian and tireless critic of Communist authoritarians)

At a United Nations forum December 7, 1988, Mikhail Gorbachev, leader of the Soviet Union, repudiated the Socialist dogma advocated by Karl Marx and Charles Darwin. Even now, many academics and journalists in America seem to be impacted by the Marx-Darwin propaganda. Reflecting upon the disintegration within Russia, Gorbachev said, "The compelling necessity of the principle of freedom of choice is...dear to us. The failure to recognize this...is fraught with very dire consequences." The powerful Socialist leader had been forced to acknowledge that those who reject the **sovereignty of man under God over government** run into the immutable laws of creation's nature.

This truth for life, liberty and the pursuit of happiness stands in contrast to the vacillating laws of man that lead to exploitation and cultural decay. Gorbachev's wife, Raisa, wrote, "Our society has set out on the path of renewal and of demolishing totalitarianism and the obsolete command system of administering the country." (Raisa Gorbachev, *Reminiscences and Reflections, Harper* Collins, 1991, p. 174)

Human Dignity, the Press, and Education

We would be sharing the revisionist views championed by secular militants had we been denied the right to be taught the lessons of history. The First Amendment to the United States *Constitution* provides that both parties (in this case, those who trust God, not just those who reject the knowledge of God) must be free from government interference to promote their views. This approach **in the context of history is beneficial, because competition sharpens citizen understanding**. This is the civic duty of newspapers, civic organizations, churches and education in our Republic. It is important, however, that citizens only subscribe to those newspapers and purchase textbooks that uphold and emphasize honest renditions of history. The wisdom for that freedom was paramount in the hearts and minds of the men who framed the foundational American charters.

Ernest Renan, a Pantheist with agnostic tendencies, wisely understood the historical value of Judeo-Christian Bible to his religious freedom. He warned his agnostic friends, *Let us enjoy the liberty of the sons of God, but let us take care lest we become accomplices in the diminution of virtue which would menace society if Christianity were to grow weak. What should we do without it? If Rationalism wishes to govern the world without regard to the religious needs of the soul, the experience of the French Revolution is there to teach us the consequences of such a blunder.* (Ernest Renan's appeal to his agnostic friends; David A. Norris, *Restoring Education Central To American Greatness,* iUniverse, Bloomington, Indiana, 2011, p. 120)

People can do what they wish in private, as long as it does not harm others. Those who take pleasure in vices that undermine their judgment and health are not necessarily lost forever—John 3:16. However, for those whose teachings challenge moral faith and defile the confidence of others, there are lasting consequences.

Employment as a teacher is not an unconditional right. Teacher tenure laws reflect harmful public sector collective bargaining laws and subsequent teacher union contracts that school boards are expected to sign. In Iowa, that Code is 20.1 - 20.26. Instead of protecting the students, parents, and the community, radical teachers can defy and overpower local citizen control about what is taught.

Secondly, problem teacher confidentiality protections make it a crime for school administrators to disclose problem teachers. They have been privileged to the protection of costly judicial proceedings, which shield them from accountability to the citizens who pay their salaries. Collective bargaining laws that do not allow the people's school board representatives to verify and follow a superintendent's judgment for dismissing a problem teacher, destroys both the citizens' sovereignty and democracy. The cure for injustice is not legalizing it.

In March 2008, harsh debate in the Iowa legislature brought this problem to the public's attention. Politicians, whose elections were advanced by campaign money that was received from outside the state and local teacher dues, were pushing for changes in the government public sector collective bargaining law. A section making it even harder to dismiss harmful teachers caused *grave concerns* among school administrators. Margaret Buckton, chief lobbyist for the Iowa Association of School Boards, says regarding arbitration, "Adjudicators have tended to rule in favor of the teachers." As the teachers' bargaining rights law now stands, *Attempts to remove a teacher can last years and cost hundreds of thousands of dollars.* (The Ames, Iowa *Tribune*, March 27, 2008, p. 4)

Accepting collective bargaining law was the political cost of outlawing teacher strikes, but both are very harmful. The solution is outlined in Chapter 11, starting on page 87.

After reading four chapters of my last book, *Restoring Education Central to American Greatness,* an Ames, Iowa teacher praised the book, but realized she had never been taught some very important history—the Great Reformation, the *Magna Carta,* and the *Declaration of Independence* would not exist, if people had not turned unabashedly to the impartial Judeo-Christian God of creation.

Chapter 7

Freedom is the Right to Take Responsibility; Tyranny of Big Government is the Price of Being a Serf

Friedrich A. Hayek published *The Road to Serfdom* in 1944. He understood the inevitable outcomes associated with government by hierarchical planners. Governments controlled for and by the people's representative are NO match for the coercive force of governments controlled by authoritarians.

The loss of religious, economic, and political freedom and the loss of millions of innocent lives under the tyranny of Soviet socialism, self-destructed in 70 years. It is true, as Hayek says, even when central planners start out well intended. This evil cycle has continually repeated throughout history. **All that is needed to prevent such a tragic epoch is pro-God, family, and country public education, which renders hierarchical government planners powerless.**

Abraham Lincoln said, "A house divided against itself cannot stand." Teacher advocacy of In God We Trust values for citizen self-reliance is American and necessary. Secular authoritarians must remove the impartial non-sectarian God of creation, found in the *Declaraton of Indendence*, from education in order to undermine student self-reliance. Abraham Lincoln's statement parallels the words of Jesus recorded in all three synoptic gospels (Matthew, Mark, Luke). The choice is ours—restore citizen control over what is taught in behavioral studies or continue yielding to consequences of secular authoritarianiam.

Successful industry requires a free enterprise system that is not undermined by monopoly controls of a partisan union/dictatorial government, which ignores the right of the people to control their own destiny.

Taxpayer citizens established and fund the education system and hire teachers to help in the teaching process. The citizens' chain of command for controlling what is and what is not taught has been tragically disrupted, by harmful collective bargaining law and teacher job guarantees. Consequently the people's command sequence has become an even greater challenge. Teacher candidates who would challenge the citizens' authority and rule of law standards are NOT eligible, because when justice and truth are compromised there is no justice. They are, of course, free to fund their own education system, as is now done by separatists of many persuasions.

Americans were committed to a citizen's Republic, chain of command under God's authority over government. That includes parent taxpayer control over what is taught in the soft sciences. In Patrick Henry style, extremism in the defense of liberty is no vice and moderation in the pursuit of justice is no virtue. The reason this is necessary is that secular militants are just as committed to their agenda. The difference is, if we are humble and stay on God's side, we win and they lose.

The citizen's Republic, chain of command rests on their God given right to government that upholds and is subordinate to their sacred values. *Done in Convention by the Unanimous Consent of the States present the Seventeenth Day of September in the Year of our Lord one thousand seven hundred and Eighty seven and of the Independence* [Declaration of Independence 12 years earlier] *of the United States of America the Twelfth, In witness whereof We have hereunto subscribed our Names.*

The duty of school board members is to serve the community and taxpayer parents who bring the students into the world. Board members, who do not uphold teachers who are committed to the moral needs of a civil and healthy society, have failed. Buildings are only important if they are used appropriately. The superintendent has a tough job. It is not possible to serve the community without the declared support of the school board members.

The loyalty and backbone of all school administrators employed in the citizen's chain of command is important, because they will be vigorously challenged. Properly taught, new generations learn the higher authority code of ethics essential for family solidarity, civil community, and material prosperity. In that way, crimes that require costly lawyers and the courts to assess punishment are avoided.

When there is a breakdown of citizen authority, it must be corrected where the failure occurs. If a people's board representative fails to select and support a discerning school superintendent, that school board member or members should not be re-elected. If, at the superintendent level, bad teachers are being hired, that administrator should be replaced on the authority of the school board, whose duty it is to represent the citizen majority. If the school board and superintendent find that a teacher is challenging the citizens' code of ethics for family solidarity and community civility, that teacher should be replaced. Continued failure to replace bad teachers will destroy the educational foundations of this nation, conceived in liberty.

The viable code of ethics is the result of education, not force. The following is from the Grand Jury Presentment previously cited.

> *Those who place their present faith and future hope in law enforcement to conduct [guide] humanity to brighter times ignore a fundamental psychological truth. It is impossible to superimpose an effective code of ethics through compulsion. Police force provides nothing more corrective than temporary control of faulty behavior traceable to education's failure to implant established knowledge of morality and the precepts of individual responsibility.*

Good laws protect all citizens, including teachers' rights to fund and support political candidates they choose. **Laws allowing teacher unions to impose dues on a politically diverse group of teachers, and use their dues to elect politicians committed to the union's secular agenda, is a violation of representative government.**

> This violation of citizen rights reminds one of authoritarian graduate methods [faculty independence from the people who finance education for civil society]. Academic freedom became *a cause celebre* [highly controversial]. Of course, it is controversial. To think that the Dean of a soft science, political, education, social, or behavioral studies department would be independent from meaningful supervision of the chief school administrator, the Board of Regents, and the people elected legislators is irrational. What should such consequent situation be called in the American Republic?

John S. Brubacher and Willis Rudy
Higher Education Transition
New York, Harper and Row, 1958
Chapter 15, Academic Freedom

Who has academic freedom, the parent/taxpayer or the teacher? Is the parent, who once had academic freedom, now to be deprived because a teacher was hired? Most agree that anyone can teach what he pleases on his own, but must not [take advantage of his own] academic freedom by robbing taxpayers of their freedom to direct public education in the public's interest, based upon the learning process and established knowledge, (Grand Jury, previously cited). Perhaps we need go no farther to provide a front seat for the ageless principles to education in university and college classrooms. I am told that they dominate lower level government public schools.

It also appears to be criminal to force a community to spend months and tens of thousands of dollars for lawyers to debate a teacher employment privilege, for what the school taxpayer majority sees as a violation of decent standards. Call it what you want. But allowing a sectarian union to override citizen control for what government education teaches as a code of ethics has staggering international consequences.

To earn employment, teachers are duty bound to support the school administrator who is employed by the citizens to superintend the quality of education acceptable to taxpaying parent employers. **This involves responsibility at three levels.**

1. **Taxpayer parents** must sacrifice and pay both the administrator and teachers for their employment.

2. The **school board members** elected by the people have the responsibility to choose a school administrator who in turn will select teachers that can teach the hard

sciences. Every bit as important is the duty of school board members to support the superintendent's concern for classroom character instruction.

To be worthy of taxpayer funding, teachers will uphold and honor the role of parents and *In God We Trust*, the official motto of the United States. A good school board and superintendent will continually encourage teachers to set a good example, to oppose moral revisionism, and reject any hint of instruction that could justify enmity or hatred between the sexes and races.

3. America is a *for, by, and of the people* Republic. Teacher candidates have the duty to be honest when declaring their support for traditional American family, human dignity, and civil community standards. Teachers are employed by taxpaying parent citizens who pay their teacher salaries and maintain the school property. Most parents who object to American Judeo-Christian education traditions, kindly opt their children out of assemblies where prayer or some similar activity occurs. Parents who object to *In God We Trust* assemblies and demand that atheistic secular education be imposed on all students fit the definition of totalitarian or fascist authoritarians. Avoiding oppression of this kind caused tens of millions of immigrants from around the globe to seek refuge in America.

If citizens learn what has caused the precipitous education decline, things will change. The people will then elect legislators committed to replacing harmful collective bargaining laws and restoring the right of school boards and superintendents to dismiss harmful and uncooperative teachers without fear of tenured secular militants. The good teacher majority can then emphasize their love for American foundations, *In God We Trust*, family, and country without fear.

The previously quoted Grand Jury emphasized that *Our soldier boys have been dying for this ideal. Education as never before should clearly teach it. So say we.* (Boston Massachusetts, Boston Record, edition January 7, 1969. Reported Ames, Iowa *Tribune*, Editorial Page, January 14, 1969.)

Chapter 8

People Can Not Fight Cancer When in Denial

Secular militants opposed to teaching moral absolutes that reflect the public norm for civil decency are serving the Enemy of responsible self-rule and liberty.

At a sizable parent-teacher meeting in 1975, my wife and I were rightly warned from the platform, "We do not teach morality in this school." (Opinion article, Ames, Iowa *Tribune*, September 25, 1992, A8) It was instantly apparent to me that the school system had gone seriously astray and that we must pay a second education tax and send our daughter to a private Christian school. When properly explained, our daughter fully understood and she matured to be a golden gem. When the news came out that she would not be back for the next school year, several teachers came to her and expressed understanding for that decision.

The [timing of] National Education Association rise is directly linked with the [now 50] year decline of American education that occurred simultaneously—not just in terms of quality, but... [increased] cost. ("How the National Education Association Corrupts Our Public Schools," *Forbes* magazine, June 7, 1993, p. 79)

The first national study of four common sexually transmitted diseases among girls and young women has found that one in four [is] infected with at least one of the diseases, U.S. health officials reported Tuesday. One in four U.S. teenage girls has STDs. The diseases, which are infections caused by bacteria, viruses, and parasites, can produce acute symptoms... and potentially fatal ectopic pregnancy...and cervical cancer. The two most common sexually transmitted diseases, or STDs, among all the participants tested were Human Papilloma Virus, at 18 percent, and Chlamydia, at four percent, according to the analysis, part of the National Health and Nutrition Examination Survey.

The Ames, Iowa *Tribune*: Lawrence K. Altman,
"One in Four U.S. Teenage Girls Have STDs, Study
Finds," *International Herald Tribune*
March 12, 2008

One of every 100 adults are in jail or prison, according to a new report documenting America's rank as the world's number one incarcerator," according to a new study by the non-partisan Pew Center. With more than 2.3 million people behind bars, the United States leads the world in both the number and percent of residents it incarcerates.

Ames, Iowa *Tribune*: David Crary
New York Associated Press, February 28, 2008

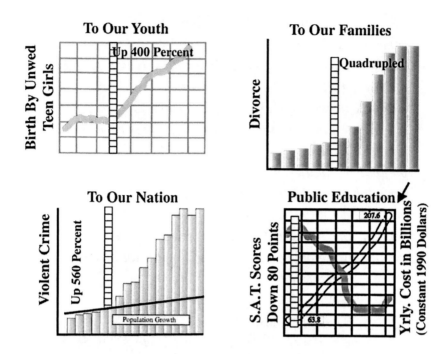

The ladder marks 1962 when the radical minority started to remove the God of creation and moral faith out of our schools. The graphs reflect public reports up to 2009.

It is a terrible mistake to employ secular exclusivists who impose a narrowness that challenges teaching the moral absolutes essential to American exceptionalism. *Nearly 40 percent of the U.S. college students engage in high-risk alcohol consumption. Each year, almost 2,000 college and university students die from alcohol-related causes. An estimated 600,000 others are injured while under the influence. Loss of life alone is reason to act, but can also lead to sexual abuse . . . damage brain development and damage impulse control.* (Dr. Jim Yong Kim, MD, PhD a Korean-American physician. Kim Chaired the Department of Global Health and Social Medicine at Harvard Medical School)

In a *Washington Post,* article, September 16, 2011, Dr. Kim writes: *As today's students evolve into engaged citizens and tomorrow's leaders, we owe it to them, to their parents and to society not to let them down.* Dr. Kim's concern that teachers for the behavioral, social, political, and law studies unabashedly emphasize morality as the supreme need for education of our day. (He is now President of the World Bank committed to reversing harmful life practices worldwide.)

Prior to the leftist's criticism of quality education and their influence over public schools starting in the late 1960s, it had not become the victim of secular philosophy. Things formerly learned in a limited way with shame in back alleys—explicit sex, the incentive of free condoms, drugs, social deviancy, and distortions of American History were rare. Even now some parents who are atheist in belief realize that people cannot violate the last six of the Biblical Ten Commandments without very serious personal consequences. The rejection of moral absolutes by instructors who are tenured has even caused some of these parents to opt out of the public school system and are home schooling.

While concerned citizens are blunt in their opposition to what secular exclusivists teach, we must not become personally judgmental and have an unforgiving spirit toward them. That is God's domain. We, too, may have been contributors to the cultural decline had we been victimized by the open-mindedness of God-rejecting education. When we fail to be forgiving, we risk poisoning our own mind, will, and emotion, thinking we are hurting the offender.

The English Language

The secular war against the God of creation is also a war against the dictionary and family. It is well documented that the Bible was the benchmark for word meanings when crafting the *Constitution of the United States.* Writers of the *Constitution* wisely left theological interpretations to the public and churches. While avoiding church theology, they were unanimous in basing foundational American charters on moral law that supports the God-honoring family and lessons of history presented by Scripture.

I was prepared at the previously mentioned Grand Jury, for the anger by radicals when they read the Presentment. What surprised me, however, was that some in academia quite sincerely complained that they could not understand the Report. Apparently, they were unable to understand the meaning of the English language used by the Grand Jury. Although printing the Presentment in the *Iowa State Daily* was the right thing to do, it did not help their radical cause, because most of the readers understood the English used by the Grand Jury.

Noah Webster (1758–1843), a contributor to the *Constitution* and widely acknowledged as the most influential educator for over a hundred years, unabashedly proclaimed his conversion to Christ during a campus revival at Yale. Webster was fluent in several languages. He finished the *American Dictionary of the English Language* in 1828. Paralleling the references to the Bible by the delegates to the

Noah Webster

Constitutional Convention, Webster often included Bible meaning to words for reliability. When meanings are twisted, words become a weapon for the enemies of man's capacity for responsible self-rule and liberty.

In past times, the word *secular* had been used to distinguish non-church governments from church governments within the context of respect for creation's God and moral law. Professors, known for rejecting God's standards that uphold life and dignity, began calling themselves **secular** humanists. Dominance of their twisted meaning for the word *secular* in textbooks now supports the atheistic rule over men.

What is one of the first things Karl Marx and his Communist friends did when they achieved control in Russia? They took religious freedom with the Bible out of education and instituted a worldwide propaganda war against the cohesiveness of marriage and the family. How else to best destroy a society? It is important to point out that some secularists respect the consciences of others and agree with natural law morality.

The examples of secular *Political Correctness* which follow are shocking. Any instruction remotely resembling the examples of leftist education Political Correctness serves to destroy the family and civil society. The following is from the *Phyllis Schlafly Report,* April 2004. Phyllis Schlafly has a superb background in the law, which is used in her reports.

> ***Everything is political.*** *All academic subjects must be seen through the prism of gender and race oppression, including history, literature, social relationships, and even private conservation.*
>
> ***Victimology.*** *Every group is entitled to claim minority status as victims, except white males and Christians.*
>
> ***Multiculturalism.*** *That's a code word for the false notion that Western Civilization is bad and every other group, whether civilized or not, is superior.*

71

Having sex with anybody, any time, is OK and may not be criticized. Dating is out; hooking up is in. The social acceptance of pre-marital and homosexual sex and activism is non-negotiable.

Tolerance. That's a code word meaning tolerance for the [leftist] Politically Correct views [not traditional American values]. Tolerance requires conformity to [their] P.C. views and hundreds of colleges have speech codes.

Christianity is Politically Incorrect. In some colleges, students are not permitted to turn in papers that identify historical dates as B.C. (Before Christ) or A.D. (Anno Domini).

Deception in the hard sciences, such as math and physics, is difficult because the outcome is instant. Great harm can occur, however, when secularized interpretations of a soft science are promoted, because the damage done usually appears later. The soft sciences include literature, journalism, political science, life origins biology, history, law studies, religion, social studies, arts, and psychology. To be a friend of the family, community, and nation, the soft sciences must be taught from the perspective of an impartial Higher Authority, not atheistic secular correctness.

At our local university a program requiring that all students receive studies in addition to required basic courses has been instituted. This parallels the harmful change to captive student classrooms in lower level teacher tenured government school systems. A fracas started when a student complained about education cost saying that students should be allowed to choose their own extra-curricular courses. The student was right and the Professor, a political science instructor, was, in my opinion, wrong. The professor, who may be a saint for all I know, said, according to the Ames, Iowa *Tribune,* January 31, 2014, "I almost wept with laughter."

If the totalitarian idea of teacher tenure privilege and collective bargaining are not abandoned in favor of citizen control and academic freedom for competing ideas, the demise of America seems clear. I predict that those newly required university-wide required courses will, because of the secular militancy of a few tenured professors, soon include God-rejecting anti-American propaganda.

Even now a small militant cadre within the soft sciences appear to be pushing leftist political correctness campus-wide. This appears to reflect the atmospherics championed by some tenured professors in the university religion studies department. The purpose of public education **is destroyed when militant secular exclusivists, powered by government enabling controls, get the upper hand.** It is my estimate that the conspicuous campus activity by just a few tenured leftist secular instructors has cost the ISU tens of millions of dollars in donor gifts.

Readers might suggest that the Iowa Board of Regents and university presidents eliminate this captive classroom project. **That will not work.** It has been tried elsewhere. Radicals, knowing they cannot be fired, have gone ahead and taught what they very well please. **The Board of Regents, superintendents, and school boards with character side with the students and general public and seek to dismantle any and all tenure guarantees for professors in the soft sciences—thereby, empowering the good teachers, who can teach unhindered by self-righteous antagonists.**

School Board members and administrators, who are qualified, will take seriously the fact that youthful trust, inexperience, and vulnerability to exploitation require that **the learning environment be protected**. God has given mankind a wonderful mind to explore the universe, but **with one exception—we are not to defile our minds by learning the details and experiencing the snares of evil.** (Genesis 2:17; Genesis 3:13; Isaiah 5:15-16, 20; Romans 16:19; and James 1:12-17)

Regardless of where schools manage to get their funding, if it fails to advocate morality, the sanctity of marriage, parental responsibility, and the Golden Rule for treating others, **it is not public education, it is** _____ .

Chapter 9

Restoring Ageless Principles to Education

Politics includes the legitimate zone for the war of ideas, in order to decide whether hierarchical authoritarians or belief in man under God over government should remain the American way.

The citizens will take action when they learn the truth. The vast majority of school administrators and teachers respect life, family, health, and civil society. They are a treasure. They do not want the kind of tenure guarantees that power secular advocates to interrupt and twist the education of our youth.

> *No single level of education can be considered in a vacuum, good or bad. It is going on! The students of colleges are, after all, the graduates of American elementary and secondary schools. We, the adults and teachers of today, are the graduates of high school, colleges, and universities in the recent past. Not only are various levels of American education interrelated, but the problems fed back upon one another to produce a complex of relationships which affect us all and must be realized.*

In the physical sciences, a faulty practice may be found out in a matter of minutes or weeks. In professions such as medicine or architecture, failures soon become apparent and are corrected. A faulty experiment with humanity has serious consequences, because the whole society is involved and errors may not be detected for two or three generations and then be too late to reverse the impetus for disaster. The highly educated German [society accommodating a skillful but fraudulent style of leadership] is an example of just such a disaster.

Excerpt from the unanimous Grand Jury Presentment,
"Harmful Activities in Education"

Political and education fraud are much easier to detect and police, when local citizen control over education is maintained. Milton and Rose Friedman pointed out in their book, *Free to Choose*, published in 1980, that the starting point for the secular authoritarian's war against local citizen control began with very harsh criticism of what was then good education. Secular militants promised to improve education; but, of course, the more dysfunctional it has become, the more reasons for them to recycle their harmful dialog.

The Friedmans quoted Walter Lippmann who diagnosed the problem as *the sickness of an over-governed society, ... the exercise of unlimited power by men with limited minds and self-regarding prejudices is soon oppressive, reactionary, and corrupt...that there are no limits to a man's capacity to govern others and that, therefore, no limits ought to be imposed upon government...For schools, this has taken the form of denying many parents control over the kind of schooling their children receive.*

This writer's father, R. C. Norris, was a good educator who dedicated his life to the work of a county school superintendent. The trend away from local citizen control began with the move away from local schools to regional school consolidation. That would have worked, if the change had been limited to regional centers for advanced instruction in the hard sciences—mathematics, chemistry, physics laboratories, etc. (That is now working quite well—home schooled students can go to public schools part-time to access advanced studies and laboratory resources.)

When I was a boy, my father took me to a school district potluck, where school board members later separated themselves and held a meeting. When I asked him about the board meeting, he told me that there were allegations of moral impropriety by a teacher. The board investigated, found the gossip to be only hearsay, and voted to keep the teacher. Most government schools are now too large for this exact approach, but the importance of the principle remains—citizen control over the impact of education through the administrator.

Collective bargaining statutes that enable union authority to impose teacher employment guarantees cause taxpayer parents, students, and the nation to be victimized.

Local persons under the auspices of the *National Education Association*, or state and local associations, who represent union bosses in local teacher contract negotiations, often omit the word *union* from their title. The contracts upheld by the judiciary imply that teachers have the authority to determine what is taught. Implied authority encourages the few tenured radicals to disrupt the school, or do whatever it takes to keep the teacher majority and school administrator in submission.

Chapter 10

Citizen Action for Government Policy Changes

James Madison

James Madison served as the fourth president of the United States (1809–1817) and is considered the principle author of the United States *Constitution.* Madison was responsible for writing the first ten amendments to the *Constitution,* also known as the *Bill of Rights.* In 1788, Madison wrote a third of the Federalist Papers. Taken as a whole they are believed to be the most reliable account that sets forth the meaning and intent for the written *Constitution.*

James Madison wrote an essay, *Who Are the Keepers of the People's Liberties?* Here is an excerpt.

Although all men are born free, and all nations might be so, yet too true it is, that slavery has been the general lot of the human race. Ignorant—they have been cheated;

asleep—they have been surprised; divided—the yoke has been forced upon them. But what is the lesson? That because the people may betray themselves, they ought to give themselves up, blindfolded, to those who have an interest in betraying them? Rather conclude that the people ought to be enlightened, to be awakened, to be united.

The *Constitution* and the free exercise of religion apply just as much inside public schools as it does anywhere else. Religion has been defined as *a strongly held belief about the origin, meaning and purpose of life*. Religious freedom in education means that hired teachers agree to teach students about the harmful consequences which follow immoral lifestyles. Allowing the poison of anti-God rhetoric to undermine belief in foundational American values is intolerable. Teacher candidates found to encourage experimentation with immoral diversities should, by law, be rejected from employment.

News organizations have the duty to protect the right of their reporters to keep the identity of news sources confidential. This is   because the promoters of immoral education diversities may seek to harm the reputation of the news sources. Darkness hates light. Without investigative news reports about events detrimental to the traditional family, human dignity, and community, the citizens cannot see the need for action.

Responsible use of freedom of the press and the freedom for alternative education providers is foundational. When business people purchase advertising in a newspaper, they are funding more than advertising. Their advertising dollars help offset newspaper opinion page costs.

In 1977, the Ames business community was confronted with the anti-free-enterprise opinions promoted by the then, Ames, Iowa *Tribune*

Opinion Editor. Addressing several business owners, I said that the *Tribune* has the right to promote what they wish, but we also have the right to advertise wherever we want to advertise. Within a few minutes the decision was made by the business people to quit advertising in the *Tribune*.

Within two months the message came back to us, "We respect your concern." The Ames, Iowa *Tribune* has been supportive of the American free enterprise system since that time. Shortly before a new advertising alternative had been developed, the business people decided to advertise again in the *Tribune*.

The *Tribune* news and their *Story County Sun* are doing a good job, considering the budget restraints caused by Internet news competition. Many conservatives and moderates, however, rightly believe that more local opinion page articles are needed— especially those which focus on the benefits from classroom instruction that emphasize moral absolutes and their value to the traditional family, human dignity, and community.

Opinion page managers do not own the truth. There is a far greater percent of conservatives and moderates in and around university campuses than some believe. Opinion page imbalance that cheats readers from the opportunity to see the conservative side of political dialog causes readers to be marginalized. The following are like-minded conservative writers covering national issues: Charles Krauthammer, Thomas Sowell, Laura Ingraham, and George Will. Input by just one of these, published regularly, with more local citizen opinions, would balance the host of secular partisan propagandists.

The inclusion of God-rejecting writers by opinion page managers is important. They are good at pointing out the weakness of conservative and moderate presentations, which causes important re-evaluations. Also readers can see how people on the left couch their interpretations for student consumption. Two of the very best opinion articles were recently submitted by local citizens. One, a Christian pastor explained orthodox commonality among different Bible believing church denominations. Another, written by a liberal emphasized the need for more investigative reporting. How true!

One of the most effective approaches for the prevention of crime are cameras that disclose what happens on our streets and in places where business is conducted. Does the possibility of the moral defilement of students' minds by a few clever secular exclusivists in the captive government classrooms justify cameras? I am not advocating cameras for the classroom, but it is going to happen.

The power of cameras in the classroom is not just uncovering crimes. Communities have some very important standards that are not punishable by law. If a tenured teacher minority does not respect and uphold those standards, continued deterioration of vital cultural statistics among students are inevitable. The reason cameras will be used is that some parents understand what has been going on and they are irate.

Another reason there will be cameras is that modern technology makes cameras easy to hide. Some students who are beneficiaries of moral training at home, Sunday school, and church attendance, come home very upset. I know of one instance where the student asked his parents, who are very prominent in our community, for permission to express his concern to the principal and they gave that permission. That student did go to the principal, but what can the school principal do when the teacher has an employment guarantee? Nothing. Who are we to protect—the students and our nation or harmful teachers?

Reports of flagrant violations of community standards by teachers need to be verifiable. There should not be any criticism or false charges, such as any made against good teachers caught taking a strong moral stand or criticizing leftist's political correctness in the classroom. I have no doubt that The Ames *Tribune* will respect concrete reports of critically verifiable news. The public outcry will cause union-teacher tenure granting lawmakers to be identified and not be re-elected.

The problem is further accented by some of the teacher union contracts which school boards and administrators are expected to approve. Union representatives have excessive school building access authority. Presumably, they do not have time for a daily walk down the hall during school activity or the right to snoop in the administrator's personal file. Extreme school access authority for those with a militant secular agenda is bound to be intimidating to teachers who uphold human dignity, the traditional family, and community morality. Good teachers are highly valued and they deserve our protection.

When treated fairly by the media reports, conservatism and moderation win. After all, conservatism and moderation rest upon the same principles that established foundational American charters. When opinion page managers prioritize opinion writers who skillfully denigrate conservative and moderate leaders, the reader's own understanding can be marginalized by the preponderance of demagoguery.

Public school students are taught by the example set by administrators and teachers in the education system. When superintendents or teachers criticize teacher dress or the use of revisionist ideology, they risk public allegations from union stalwarts that are not true. This causes the administrators and teachers to withdraw from emphasizing substantial truth that students need and have the right to know. When courageous students speak the truth in class, and some do, they risk punishment with a lowered grade.

Union tenured radicals use the same attack method to shame those who promote celebrations of Christmas. This is well-documented by several publications. One is by a Jewish author, Ben Shapiro— *Bullies: How the Left's Culture of Fear and Intimidation Silences America*. Another by S. E. Cupp, an atheist who values the Christians' disposition to do good, and supports religious liberty—*Losing Our Liberty: The Liberal Media's Attack On Christianity*.

Precisely because of the obvious potential for abuse, even labor union advocates like AFL-CIO President George Meany and Franklin D. Roosevelt viewed unionization of the public employees as unthinkable. (Peter Brimelow and Leslie Spencer, "How the National Education Association Corrupts Our Public Schools," *Forbes* magazine, June 7, 1993)

Rabbi Soul Roth explains the tragic mental disconnect that occurs when creation's God, even Christmas, is forced out of the school building. He calls it *functional segregation*. Students are victims of mentally crippling education that substitutes men for creation's God. Secular teachers and Darwin's view for the origin of life get the credit for the complex marvels, function, and beauty that only our Almighty God could have made.

Furthermore, science becomes *knowledge, apart from moral values*. Consequently, *Morality has been steadily eroding in America*. Morals are not just good ideas, they are founded in a perfect understanding of man's nature. The truth about man's nature is only known to the

God of creation. Functional segregation in classrooms is harmful to religious faith, hence making the family and community *irrelevant.* (Rabbi Soul Roth is an author and professor at New York's Yeshiva University, www. 5as.org/index.php/who-we-are/who-s-who).

Parents, teachers and others who advocate moral absolutes, such as thou shall not steal, or tell lies, and explain why, are not prudes. Morality is the backbone for every aspect of civil community and industry. It is the secular enemies of the family and Higher Authority who have gone bonkers.

The teacher majority knows what union tenure contract controls over classrooms has done to the mind-set of students, but many parents do not. Studies show that a significantly higher percentage of public school teachers send their children to private schools than do non-teacher parents. *The percentage of public school teachers nationwide who are choosing to protect their own children by sending them to private schools is over twice the rate of non-teacher parents."* (*World,* August 5, 1995) *More than half of parents with children in public schools ...would send their children to private schools if they could afford to.* (The Ames, Iowa *Tribune,* October 11, 1995)

Abigail Adams, wife of John Adams, the second president of the United States, was a strong advocate for women's rights. John had written her saying that the newly passed *Declaration of Independence will be the most memorable epoch in the history of America. I am apt to believe that it will be celebrated by succeeding generations as the great anniversary festival. It ought to be commemorated as the Day of Deliverance by solemn acts of devotion to God Almighty. It ought to be solemnized with pomp and parade, with shows, games, sports, guns, bells, bonfires, and illuminations from one end of this continent to the other from this time forward forever more.*

In a letter Abigail sent to their young son, John Quincy, who would later become our sixth president, she emphasized:

Great learning and superior abilities, should you ever possess them, will be of little value and small Estimation, unless Virtue, Honor, Truth, and integrity are added to them. Adhere to those religious Sentiments and principles that were early installed into your mind and remember that you are accountable to your Maker for all your words and actions. Let me enjoin it upon you to attend constantly and steadfastly to the precepts and instructions of your Father as you value the happiness of your Mother and your own welfare. His care and attention to you render many things unnecessary for me to write which I might otherwise do, but the inadvertency and Heedlessness of youth, requires line upon line and precept upon precept, and when enforced by the joint efforts of both parents will I hope have a due influence upon your Conduct, for dear as you are to me, I had much rather you should have found your Grave in the ocean you have crossed, or any untimely death crop you in your Infant years, rather than see you an immoral profligate or Graceless child.

Abigail Adams, Letter to John Quincy Adams
Butterfield Adams Family Correspondence, Safari
June 10, 1778

Repeating the foundation for quality education, *For the first [now over 340 years] of this country's history, religion and education were intimate and interdependent. Religious competition does stir controversy, but religious freedom enriches rather than impoverishes public policy and the education process.*

Edward Scott Gaustad, *A Religious History of America*,
Professor of History
University of California, Riverside

There are a very few public school systems in Iowa, where taxpaying parents successfully exercise their sovereignty and control in what is being taught in the behavioral, social and history subjects. For their protection, the very few that I know of are not being identified. How do these communities maintain local citizen control? **It is the result of the conscientious effort promoted by news editors, churches, public service, and school boards to keep the school system clean and protect it from progressive worldly liberals.** Americans cherish diversity, but reject the immoral diversities advocated by the professors of political correctness.

Chapter 11

Vital Changes in Our Laws Needed for Restoring Ageless Principles to Education

Almost every opportunity a person will have in his/her life is affected by the quality of the education they receive.

Unions with limits, which require them to compete with other suppliers for buyer acceptance, can be helpful. Teacher tenure guarantees enabled by the teachers' union's monopoly, however, have proven to be the enemy of moral standards, which empower the traditional family and civil community.

The following is from the Grand Jury Presentment previously cited.

> *Those who place their present faith and future hope in laws enforcement to conduct [guide] humanity to brighter times ignore a fundamental psychological truth. It is impossible to superimpose an effective code of ethics through compulsion. Police force provides nothing more corrective than temporary control of faulty behavior traceable to education's failure to implant established knowledge of morality and the precepts of individual responsibility...*

Our soldier boys have been dying for this ideal. Education should clearly teach it. Even in imperfection it has achieved greatness for Americans unparalleled in history. Something alien philosophies envy, but do provide...

*Regents' policy changes which will sufficiently define and implement the **elimination of moral pollution** by faculty and paid speakers and will by all suitable means encourage moral improvement...*

Constitution of the State of Iowa, Article IX,
2nd School, Sec. 3

We do not need open-minded atheistic secular education. The question for any people in trouble is, can integrity be restored? Some years ago, George E. LaMore. Jr., Chairman of the Division of Humanities at Iowa Wesleyan College, spoke to business men and women in Ames regarding the existence of education absolutes that support families, human dignity, and limited government. Concerned about the retreat from traditional American values in behavioral and history studies, Professor LaMore said, "We are up to here in education and got ourselves into this mess." (I interrupt this thought briefly to write that the fault rests with a few secular militants empowered by harmful collective bargaining laws and union contracts that impose teacher tenure guarantees.) Professor LaMore continues, "...shortage is not brains, but a shortage of integrity. Our problem is not one of knowledge, but one of morality."

Our Regents are powerless however to do this, because of current collective bargaining law and subsequent professor and teacher tenure guarantees. Paul Harvey and several newspapers throughout the nation supported the Grand Jury Presentment using above three quotes.

The superior ability of non-government public school systems is clear. The corrections which follow are needed to retain taxpayer support which are also needed to save the government school system.

1.) Correct government-public sector collective bargaining law that denies taxpaying parents authority over unions now powered to dictate teacher employment. This will leverage the citizen's *Hope for America*. In 1959, the *First public sector collective bargaining law, [was] passed in Wisconsin*. This law, now common throughout the nation, has proven to be very detrimental. Harry C. Veryser, now chair of the economics and finance department of Walsh College, reportedly joked *that the union's ruthless and insatiable drive for power and perquisites should earn the new name: the National Extortion Association*. (Quotes, Peter Brimelow and Leslie Spencer, *How the National Education Association Corrupts Our Public Schools*, *Forbes* magazine, June 7, 1993, p. 72)

Cited later, California Superior Court Judge Rolf M. Treu declared *that statutes protecting teacher tenure are hurting students' chances to succeed*. Our youth are being held hostage by ignorance that has been imposed upon them.

In this book we provide a review of the citizen's chain of command for controlling how their schoolhouse tax dollars are used regarding what new generations should and should not be taught. Collective bargaining law, teacher tenure privilege, or whatever, that allows teacher contracts to override and literally destroy the citizen's chain of command structure is a crime against government of, by, and for the people.

There is now a grave need for tough penalties against teacher unions for using teachers' money as a contribution to candidates for government office. The law should punish a political candidate for accepting such money. There is also the grave need for laws that allow disclosure of violations of moral societal standards by school employees, which are certified by witnesses.

Those who support the union agenda for contracts that require hundreds of thousands of dollars and years before the people can be told the truth have done imperial damage to representative government and responsible liberty. Although great harm is being done at the public school system level, the reason is the citizen's chain of command, administrators, and teachers are being held hostage by unjust laws.

Entire books reporting injustices against students and society nationwide have been written. Superior Court Judge Rolf M. Treu was right about the great harm caused teacher tenure law.

If an employee in the business community committed such an egregious violation against moral business standards, that employee would be fired immediately, even if a substitute replacement had to be employed. What happens to our youth is far more important than a business transaction. Home school moms, by the way, make very good substitute teachers.

No one man, however brilliant or well-informed, can come in one lifetime to such fullness of understanding as to safely judge and dismiss the customs or institutions of his society, for these are the wisdom of generations after centuries of experiment in the laboratory of history. A youth boiling with hormones will wonder why he should

*not give full freedom to his sexual desires; and if he is
unchecked by custom, morals, or laws, he may ruin his
life before he matures sufficiently to understand that sex
is a river of fire that must be banked and cooled by a
hundred restraints if it is not to be consumed in chaos in
both the individual and the group.*

Will and Ariel Durant, *The Lessons of History*
New York: Simon and Schuster, 1968, pages 35–36

(This magnifies the great benefit of a lifelong, peaceful marriage
between man and a woman and the benefit to the children who live
with their father and mother.)

The urgent need for an informed citizenry is the reason for writing
this book. Judicial willingness to advance unjust laws that destroy
the people's right to control education are dragging America down,
down, down. On June 10, 2014, a courageous California, Superior
Court Judge Rolf M. Treu declared that *statutes protecting teacher
tenure are hurting students' chances to succeed.* Persons like Judge
Treu need the support of the people.

Commenting on the action, James Ryan, Dean of Harvard
University's graduate school of education pointed out *that the
decision explicitly called on the state legislature to fix the destructive
and **unconstitutional** statutes at issue.* He said, *This has a long way
to go before it's over in California and it hasn't even started yet in the
other states.* (Los Angeles AP and several other news outlets)

Politicians, let's go to work for the Iowa taxpayers. Readers of this
in other states, encourage your politicians to make the corrections
needed. By restoring the authority of taxpaying parents and the

school administrators they hire to control teacher selection, a militant secular minority will not be there to demonize and discourage good teachers, who would emphasize standards for strong childbearing marriages, communities, and public morality in general.

2.) Professors and lower level government public school teachers should no longer be allowed to control decisions outside their field of expertise. Tyranny is inevitable when the convergence of religious or political monopoly destroys the academic freedom of other departments. When there is a violation of First Amendment law, the consequences can be devastating. In other words, a religious studies department or political science department should not be allowed to dictate or enforce curriculum changes in other fields of education, or dictate and enforce student memorial union policies.

3.) Qualified teachers deserve good salaries. Establish a non-partisan system to advance teachers' salaries based upon comparable services provided by similar organizations for employee group benefits, insurance options, etc.

4.) Restore the citizen sovereignty and authority of taxpaying parents, by empowering them to access education tax dollars to cover tuition costs for non-government schools, public or private, that honor their family values.

5.) Establish conspiracy laws, which subject proven actionable proceedings by individuals to subvert the Federal government application of First Amendment and Tenth Amendment protections against tyranny of the mind, a crime. Such is a crime against citizen sovereignty and local control—the states being considered local entities. This does not, of course, prevent federal prosecution of crimes such as racial injustice, civil rights violations, bodily harm, murder, fraud, and violations of property ownership, etc. Establishment of federal government tyranny of the mind is treacherous, because the central government is too far removed from the people for them to control. On the other side of the issue, the state's right, for instance, to permit access to the Ten Commandments in their schools and courthouses, should be clearly protected.

6.) Get more voters out to School Board elections. A study for the 1981 Iowa legislature led to a survey of Iowa County Auditors who serve as elections officers. The survey proposed that the date of school board elections be changed to occur at the same time of the general elections that have many times more participants. Just short of 90 percent of County officials returned the survey and they were unanimous in support of combining the elections. The survey results showed that in approximately 26 percent of school districts, the number of people voting was less than the number of employees of the districts and their spouses. That was not true, for instance, in the Story County school districts.

Senate File 118 sponsors for combining the elections included Senators with school board experience. It was assigned to the Senate's Subcommittee on Education on January 22, 1981 and killed there. The proposal was supported by the Des Moines Blacks' political organization. The argument used to kill the proposed law was the difficulty of servicing the school districts, whose boundaries are different from local general election districts. The county elections officers who returned the survey were unanimous in support of the idea and, presumably, they did not mind preparing ballots for districts with differing boundaries.

7). Encourage the establishment of neighborhood study groups that dig out the facts. These groups could do well to monitor the way local and state legislators and school board members have been voting on the above and share their observations. *Wisdom* is knowing what to **do**, *virtue* is **doing it**.

Chapter 12

You and I Are the Link to Victory—
Local Citizen Communicators

When we proceed as the citizen information and Alert Committees did in 1775, '76 and '78, our families, students and communities will be victorious.

Motivation for actively promoting *Hope for America*:

1.) Respect for the family and parenting duties restored.

2.) Elimination of harmful child abuse where it occurs in captive taxpayer funded classrooms.

3.) Free good administrators and teachers from secular militants that are protected by teacher tenure guarantees, who can twist the truth and make false charges with impunity.

4.) Advantages economically—lower prison and hospital costs by having fewer youthful victims of revisionist morality.

5.) America will have more leaders who understand America's values embedded in fundamental governing charters.

6.) Removing teacher tenure guarantees will enable school superintendents to stop what Thomas Jefferson called *tyranny of the mind* by a few teachers who influence students not yet established in their life values.

I am indebted to my parents and community for a background fitting to this endeavor. Newspapers reported the previously mentioned Grand Jury Presentment for several days nationwide. They also fairly reported leftists' anger towards the Grand Jury and me in particular. My business, which had just started in Ames, was not hurt. In fact, it grew rapidly.

Knowledge motivates. When informed, parents, grandparents, and others will join in the battle for citizen control over what is and is not taught in the behavioral studies—and what is taught as American history. With your help in this project, distribution of the Hope for America documentary will be multiplied countless times. Every parent, grandparent, education leader, pastor, business employer, and political leader in our communities should be informed. Ideas you may have for improving the presentation are most welcome.

The *Heartland Foundation, Inc.* and *Endowment to Restore Ageless Educational Principles* are citizen-partnership enabling organizations. Endow Iowa was established by the Iowa legislature to encourage citizens to invest in community service programs.

I am told that during a typical week, users of the *Heartland Foundation, Inc.* www.lastingsuccessedu.org website download the equivalent of approximately 250 350-page books. Other organizations are quoting from the material as well. As a weapon for victory, the *Hope for America* handbook documents the foundational charters that enabled America to become the greatest nation on earth.

Thank you for your help. The story is told about John Chapman, born in 1774, who later traveled through the American colonies giving out apple seeds. To find where John's work had changed things for the better, all people had to do was travel and look for apple trees.

Sincerely,

David A. Norris,
Unsalaried President and Founder of Heartland Foundation, Inc. and Manager of the Endowment to Restore Ageless Educational Principles Agency

PO Box 1766, Ames, Iowa 50010
dnorr@att.net

By Restoring Education — We Secure the Future

Helping Others Helping Us!

Distribution of the *Hope for America* victory handbook
by relatively few . . . multiplied
many times . . . can reach millions.

Making it so everyone can participate,
there are three ways to **Help.**

Helping by Check or Money Order:

☐   Enclosed is my federal tax-deductible gift to **Heartland Foundation, Inc.,** P.O. Box 1766, Ames, Iowa 50010. Your gift is very much appreciated and will help to advance the *Hope for America* **cause.** You will receive an acknowledgment for tax preparation filings.

◯$450   ◯$300   ◯$200   ◯$100   ◯$50   ◯Other: $ _____

☐   Please find enclosed my generous contribution **to the Citizens' Endowment to Restore Ageless Educational Principles,** P.O. Box 1766, Ames, Iowa 50010. In addition to the non-profit federal public service tax-deduction, these gifts are eligible for the 25% Endow Iowa Tax Credit for Iowa taxpayers. This Iowa tax credit was instituted by Iowa legislators. Donors will be contacted by the Story County Community Foundation personnel for details relating to the Endow Iowa Tax Credit filings. Your gift is very much appreciated and will help to advance the *Hope for America* **cause.**

◯$10,000   ◯$7,000   ◯$3,000   ◯$1,000   ◯Other: $ _____

Deductible gifts of farmland and other properties are possible.

Contact us if you have questions. David A. Norris, P.O. Box 1766, Ames, Iowa 50010, dnorr@att.net, or call 515-232-1054. Contact the Story County Foundation office at kbolluyt@storycountyfoundation.org or call 515-232-9200.

Please keep our gift confidential: Yes____ No____.

Donor _____ Address _____

Phone_____ E-mail_____ Other _____

Helping Others Helping Us!

Distribution of the *Hope for America* victory handbook
by relatively few . . . multiplied
many times . . . can reach millions.

You Can Provide Leadership — as a Distributor of
Hope for America
to friends, neighbors, associates, clubs or others.

6 – 49 copies *Hope for America* .... $7.25 each
50 – 99 copies.. $6.84 each
100 – 499 copies.................................... $6.17 each
500 + copies... $5.80 each

Larger volume discounts are available. Contact us.

Free shipping for orders of $75 or more.
Shipping is $4.99 for orders under $75.

Call or email us at:
Faithful Life Publishers
Phone: 888-720-0950
info@FaithfulLifePublishers.com

It May Be Possible
to obtain a contract to republish this entire book,
verbatim, and add your name with a patriotic statement
approved by Heartland Foundation, Inc. Faithful Life
Publishers, that controls the text, will print these for you.
Contact David A. Norris at dnorr@att.net.

David A. Norris is the non-salaried founder and president
of Heartland Foundation, Inc., chartered in February, 1981.

Appendix A

A Scientist Reflects on Religious Belief

Dr. Allan Sandage

Q. Can the existence of God be proved?

I should say not with the same type of certainty that we ascribe to statements such as "the earth is in orbit about the sun at a mean distance of 93 million miles, making a complete journey in 365.25 days," or "genetic information is coded in long protein strings of DNA that, in cells of a particular individual, replicate during mitosis, and in reproduction unite with DNA from another individual to produce the hereditary similarity of progeny with their parents, etc." The enormous success of modern science is undeniable in producing such facts, which have a strong ring of certainty, and this success simply cannot be ignored.

Proofs of the existence of God have always been of a different kind—a crucial point to be understood by those scientists who will only accept results that can be obtained via the scientific method. God can never be proved to them for that reason. (Those who deny God at the outset by some form of circular reasoning will never find God.) Science illumines brightly, but only a part of reality.

The classical proofs of God by Anselm and by Aquinas via *natural theology* do not give the same type of satisfaction as proofs of propositions arrived at by the method of science. To the modern mind they seem contrived. Nevertheless, they were sufficient for Pascal to finally approach *his* certainty in God's existence by preparing his mind for God's necessity, if the world is to make ultimate sense. After that preparation, he simply could then abandon the God of natural theology and of the philosophers, and could at last will himself to faith by leaping across the abyss, from the edge of reason on this side of the chasm. For those who have experienced this way to God, I would say that God's existence has been proved beyond doubt for them.

Q. Must there necessarily be a conflict between science and religion?

In my opinion, no, if it is understood that each treats a different aspect of reality. The Bible is certainly not a book of science. One does not study it to find the intensities and the wavelengths of the Balmer spectral lines of hydrogen. But neither is science concerned with the ultimate spiritual properties of the world, which are also real.

Science makes explicit the quite incredible natural order, the interconnections at many levels between the laws of physics, the chemical reactions in the biological processes of life, etc. But science can answer only a fixed type of question. It is concerned with the what, when, and how. It does not, and indeed cannot, answer within its method (powerful as that method is), *why*.

Why is there something instead of nothing? Why do all electrons have the same charge and mass? Why is the design that we see everywhere so truly miraculous? Why are so many processes so deeply interconnected?

But we must admit that those scientists that want to see design *will* see design. Those that are content in every part of their being to live as materialistic reductionalists (*as we must all do as scientists in the laboratory, which is the place of the practice of our craft*) will never admit to a mystery of the design they see, always putting off by one step at a time, awaiting a reductionalist explanation for the present unknown. But to take this reductionalist belief to the deepest level and to an indefinite time into the future (and it will always remain indefinite) when "science will know everything" is itself an act of faith which denies that there can be anything unknown to science, even in principle. But things of the spirit are not things of science.

There need be no conflict between science and religion if each appreciates its own boundaries and if each takes seriously the claims of the other. The proven success of science simply cannot be ignored by the church. But neither can the church's claim to explain the world at the very deepest level be dismissed. If God did not exist, science would have to (and indeed has) invent the concept to explain what it is discovering at its core. Abelard's 12th century dictum "Truth cannot be contrary to truth. The findings of reason must agree with the truths of scripture, else the God who gave us both has deceived us with one or the other" still rings true.

If there is no God, nothing makes sense. The atheist's case is based on a deception they wish to play upon themselves that follows already from their initial premise. And if there is a God, he must be true both to science and religion. If it seems not so, then one's hermeneutics (either the pastor's or the scientist's) must wrong.

I believe there is a clear, heavy, and immediate responsibility for the church to understand and to believe in the extraordinary results and claims of science. Its success is simply too evident and visible to ignore. It is likewise incumbent upon scientists to understand that science is incapable, because of the limitations of its method by reason alone, to explain and to understand *everything* about reality. If the world must simply be understood by a materialistic reductionalist nihilism, it would make no sense at all. For this, Romans 1:19-21 seems profound. And the deeper any scientist pushes his work, the more profound it does indeed become.

Q. Do recent astronomical discoveries have theological significance?

I would say not, although the discovery of the expansion of the Universe with its consequences concerning the possibility that astronomers have identified the creation event does put astronomical cosmology close to the type of medieval natural theology that attempted to find God by identifying the first cause. Astronomers may have found the first effect, but not, thereby, necessarily the first cause sought by Anselm and Aquinas.

Nevertheless, there are serious scientific papers discussing events very shortly after the big bang creation (ex nihilo?) out of which all the types of matter that we know (baryons, electrons, photons, etc.) were made, and in what quantities. Even the creation of matter is said now to be understood. Astronomical observations have also suggested that this creation event, signaled by the expansion of the Universe, has happened only once. The expansion will continue forever, the Universe will not collapse upon itself, and therefore this type of creation will not happen again.

But knowledge of the creation is *not* knowledge of the creator, nor do any astronomical findings tell us why the event occurred. It is truly supernatural (i.e. outside our understanding of the natural order of things), and by this definition a miracle. But the nature of God is not to be found within any part of these findings of science. For that, one must turn to the scriptures, if indeed an answer is to be had within our finite human understanding.

Q. Can a person be a scientist and also be a Christian?

Yes. As I said before, the world is too complicated in all its parts and interconnections to be due to chance alone. I am convinced that the existence of life with all its order in each of its organisms is simply too well put together. Each part of a living thing depends on all its other parts to function. How does each part know?

How is each part specified at conception? The more one learns of biochemistry the more unbelievable it becomes unless there is some type of organizing principle-an architect for believers-a mystery to be solved by science (even as to *why*) sometime in the indefinite future for materialist reductionalists.

This situation of the complication and the order to function of an organism, where the sum is greater than its parts (i.e. has a higher order), becomes more astonishing every year as the scientific results become more detailed. Because of this, many scientists are now driven to faith by their very work. In the final analysis it is a faith made stronger through the argument by design. I simply do not now believe that the reductionalist philosophy, so necessary to pursue the scientific method and, to repeat, the method which all scientists must master and practice with all their might and skill in their laboratory, can explain everything.

Having, then, been forced via the route of Pascal and Kierkegaard in their need for purpose to come to the edge of the abyss of reason, scientists can, with Anselm "believe in order to understand" what they see, rather than "understand in order to believe." Having willed oneself to faith by jumping to the other side, one can pull, at first, a wee small thread across the abyss, pulling in turn a still more sturdy rope, until finally one can build a bridge that crosses in reverse the chasm that connects the sides of life that are reason and faith. It is, then, by faith that a scientist can become a Christian, and yet remain a scientist-believing in some form of Abelard's dictum.

Without that faith there is no purpose, and without purpose all the arguments for its need drive one once again to build Pascal's bridge.

Dr. Allan Sandage, of the Observatories of the Carnegie Institution, is described as the most influential astronomer of the last half-century. Sandage is credited with founding the discipline of observational cosmology. As Edwin Hubble's star student, he took over Hubble's mission to measure the universe's expansion and, through those measurements, to determine the physics of the cosmic creation event. He is the recipient of the prize for cosmology, equivalent to the Nobel Prize, from the Swedish parliament. Dr. Allen Sandage became a Christian at the age of 50.

Appendix B

Ageless Principles and Government, Made Simple *That students might appreciate the truth about the culture* that enabled America to be an exceptional nation

I. The Issue throughout History

Americans understand the two opposing presuppositions for life, which reflect different views of reality. As one nation under God's guidance, spoken of in the American *Declaration* of 1776, the people were blessed with liberty, justice and prosperity never before achieved in world history. (See the Introduction and Chapters 1 through 5 in this book.)

The other, an atheistic exclusivist view, rejects the only hope that supports families and community exceptionalism. (See pages 9 and 52-53 of this book.) Glorified in secular manifestoes, tyranny reigns as authoritarians impose secular propaganda and overpower government by and for the people. (See pages 55-56.)

II. Hope for America - Truth Is Known and Ours to Use

Creation's God has given mankind a conscience that comprehends moral truth. Truth is resident in the Ten Commandments and the Golden Rule. The Judeo-Christian Bible is also a history book that records the outcomes associated with good and evil. (See Chapters 7 and 8.)

Opposition to murder, theft, perjury, fraud, adultery, etc. is universal. These God-given parameters protect the lives of believers. Paraphrasing Noah Webster: Individuals' consciences cause feelings, which tell them whether they are doing something that is right or morally wrong. When our minds are protected, (particularly the youth whose life values are not yet established) respect for morality prevails. (See pages 50-51.) Known as virtue, it reflects the divine element that frees man to do what is right.

III. Hope for America - Truthful Education

Our Constitutional Fathers *wisely* left theological interpretations of the Bible to the public and churches. While avoiding the conflicts of denominational doctrine, they were unanimous in basing foundational American charters and public education on moral law - the ageless principles for human dignity, the family, and representative government. The enemies of citizen self-rule sought to marginalize the understanding of new generations by eliminating the knowledge of a Higher Authority from education, celebrations of Christmas, and the media in general.

The education for American exceptionalism was briefed by Abraham Lincoln in his Second Inaugural Address, March 4, 1865. Carved in garnet on the walls of the Lincoln Memorial, he emphasized God fourteen times and quoted the Bible twice. Lincoln concluded by saying, With malice toward none, with charity for all, with firmness in the right as God gives us to see the right, let us strive on to finish the work we are in... Lincoln's message still fills the education gap of our day. (See the Introduction of this book.)

Through the 340 years of this country's history, religion and education have been intimate and interdependent. Religious competition does stir controversy; but religious freedom enriches, rather than impoverishes, public policy and the education process. (See pages 5-6)

IV. Where Does the Government (which Serves as a Tool For Liberty) Get Its Power?

1) The sovereignty of man under God over government. When amendments to the U. S. *Constitution* are honored, local and state governments can then overrule the excesses of central government servants. (See pages 13-14.)

The *Constitution of the United States* agreed to by the people, is a sovereignty of man, under God, over government contract. One of the many absolutes spelled out in the *Constitution,* which restricts government judiciary powers, is the jury system. This system requires that any defendant accused of a crime be judged by local citizens, not a government judge. No one, including the President of the United States, has the right to deny this authority, which belongs to the people. (See pages 31-33.)

The *A Nation at Risk* study published in 1983, is by far the most significant non-partisan study of public education to date. Denigrated by atheistic secular types, the report concluded: "The educational foundations of our society are presently being eroded by a rising tide...that threatens our very future as a Nation and a people. We *might well have viewed it as an act of war* against America."

The report emphasized this famous dictum by Thomas Jefferson.

> *I know no safe depository of the ultimate powers of the society but the people themselves; and if we think them not enlightened enough to exercise their control with a wholesome discretion, the remedy is not to take it from them, but to inform their discretion.*

2. The enormous bank funded by the people. Our public treasury pays for government services.

3. The Morality Test for law is essential for restricting the power of government, including government employed teachers. When switching from Common law to Case law, the morality test became passé. **Any precedent that has abandoned the natural law moral commandments for judging cases, has destroyed the judiciary as a stabilizer for civil society.** (See Chapter 3.) Unelected judges who legislate, are betraying the representative process and the Americans who created the government and pay their salaries. (See Chapters 10 through 12.)

In his July 4, 1821 oration, Secretary of State, John Quincy Adams (soon to become President) captured the foundation for American law. (See the Introduction page viii and page xiii-xiv.)

V. What Are the Tools Used by the Enemies of Society?

Happiness, man's highest aspiration, is not driven by coercion but by education, which teaches the historic principles emphasized in this book. The first four Biblical Commandments establish the mindset needed to inspire man's respect for the Creator of life, liberty, and prosperity.

The main weapons, used by enemies of citizen self-rule and liberty, are physical force and propaganda, which Jefferson called *tyranny of the mind.* Control of what is taught in the soft sciences **must** be controlled by the local citizen's chain of command. (See pages 60-62.) Permitting government employees to design behavioral, religious, political, and historical instruction always leads to deception and tyranny of the mind. This is exemplified by the moral decline among our youth in recent decades. (See Chapter 8.) Unelected judges, who legislate and condone teacher union tenure domination and undemocratic collective bargaining privileges, compare with the tragic church-state education monopoly of Medieval Europe. (See pages 6-7 and page 28, Principle # 11.)

America is at one of those historic points, which requires us to turn back to what it was that provided our success in the first place.

INDEX

CPSIA information can be obtained
at www.ICGtesting.com
Printed in the USA
FFOW05n1405050916